# Guelph Ontario and Area in Photos, Saving Our History One Photo at a Time

Photography
by Barbara Raué
2012

Series Name:
Cruising Ontario

Book 20: Guelph

Cover photo: Ontario Veterinary College

# Series Name: Cruising Ontario

# Other Books by Barbara Raue

Coins of Gold

Arrows, Indians and Love

The Life and Times of Barbara
Volume 1: Inventions That Have Enhanced My Life
Volume 2: Entertainment That I Have Enjoyed
Volume 3: East Coast Trips
Volume 4: Olympics
Volume 5: Wonders of the World
Volume 6: Caribbean Cruises
Volume 7: Animals
Volume 8: Storms

# Guelph

Guelph, known as "The Royal City, is located 100 kilometres (62 miles) west of downtown Toronto at the intersection of Highways 6 and 7. Guelph was founded on St. George's Day, April 23, 1827, the feast day of the patron saint of England. The town was named to honour Britain's royal family, the Hanoverians who were descended from the Guelfs, the ancestral family of George IV, the reigning British monarch. The first cable TV system began in Guelph with their first broadcast being the coronation of Queen Elizabeth II in 1953. The Speed and Eramosa Rivers flow through the city.

The Ontario Agricultural College, the oldest part of the University of Guelph, began in 1873 as an associate agricultural college of the University of Toronto. The Government of Ontario purchased 550 acres of land from F. W. Stone to build the college. In 1964, the Ontario Agricultural College, Ontario Veterinary College and Macdonald Institute combined to become the University of Guelph and Wellington College.

## Moffat

Moffat is located north of the 401, southeast of Guelph. We lived in Guelph from the fall of 1954 to the spring of 1956 when we moved to the outskirts of Guelph on Old York Road across from the Ontario Reformatory grounds. When the boundary of Guelph extended eastward, the name of our road became Beaumont Crescent and our house number was 18.

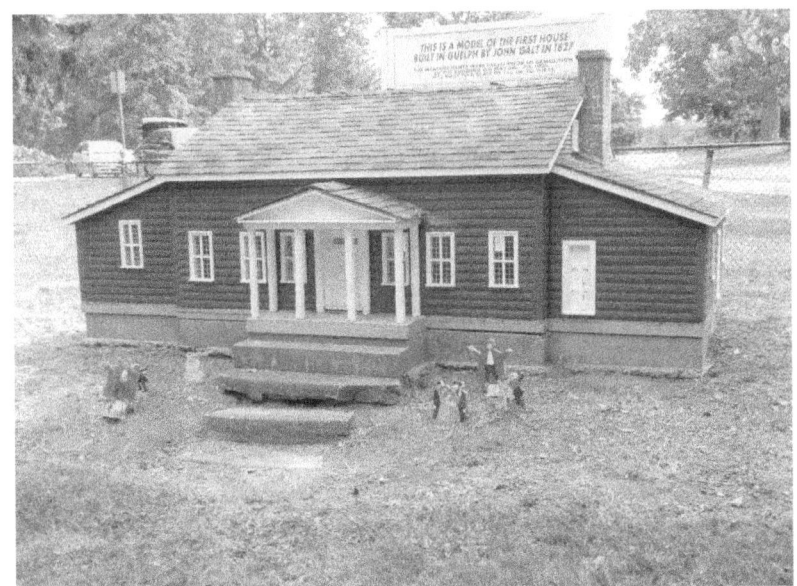

Model of the first house built in Guelph by John Galt in 1827

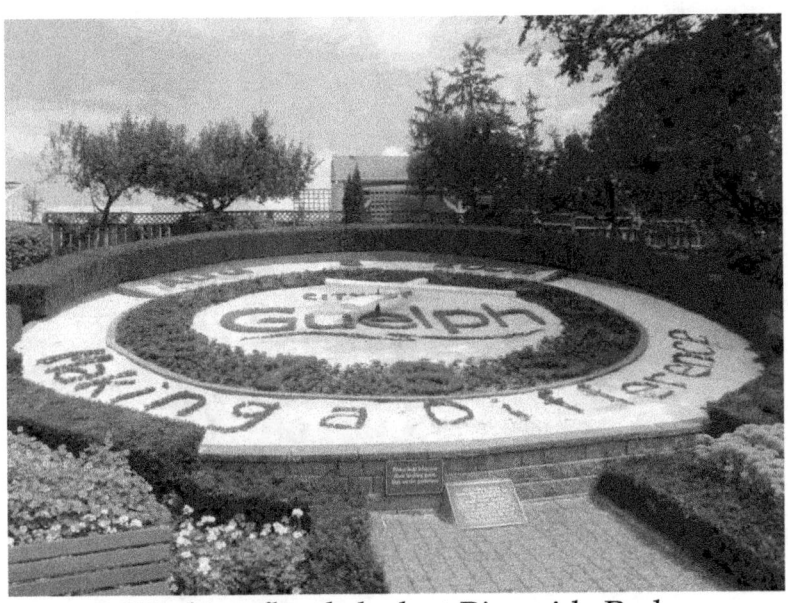

Working floral clock at Riverside Park
– the date is changed daily

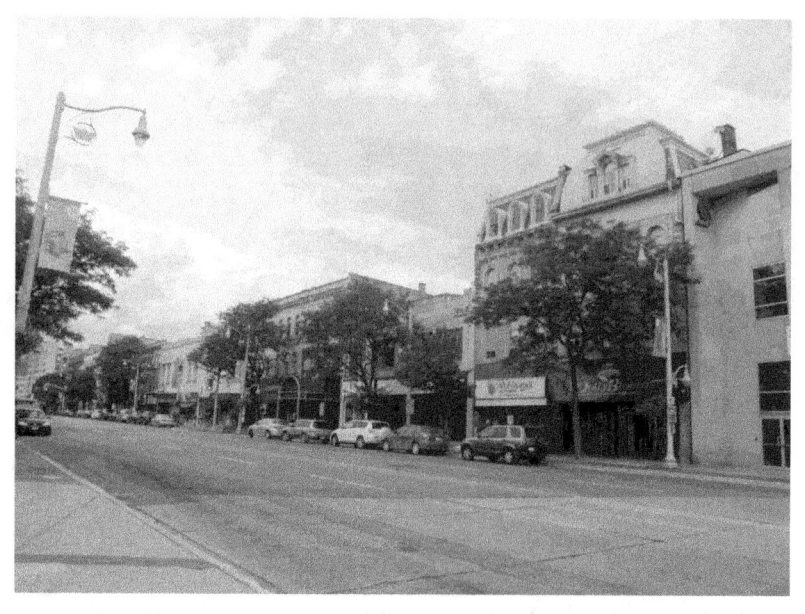

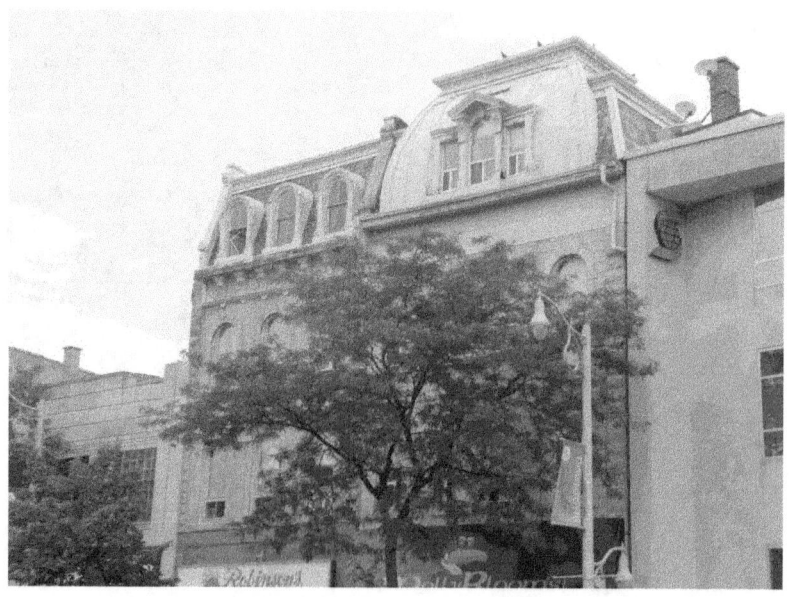

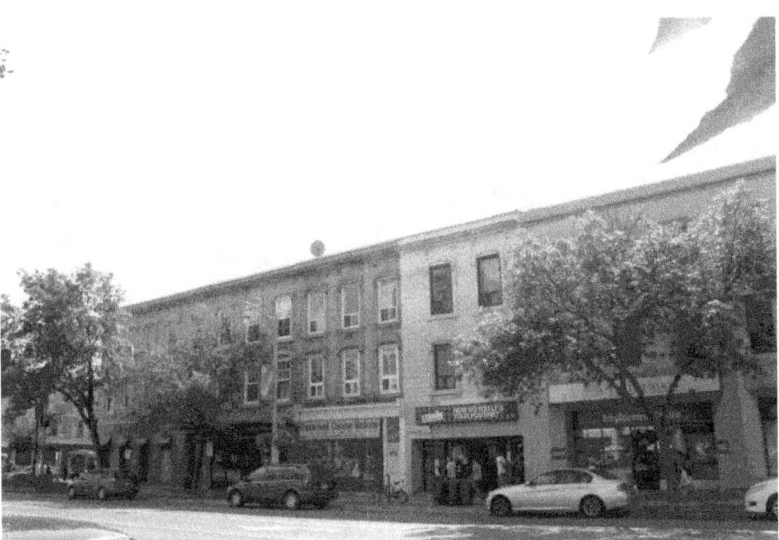

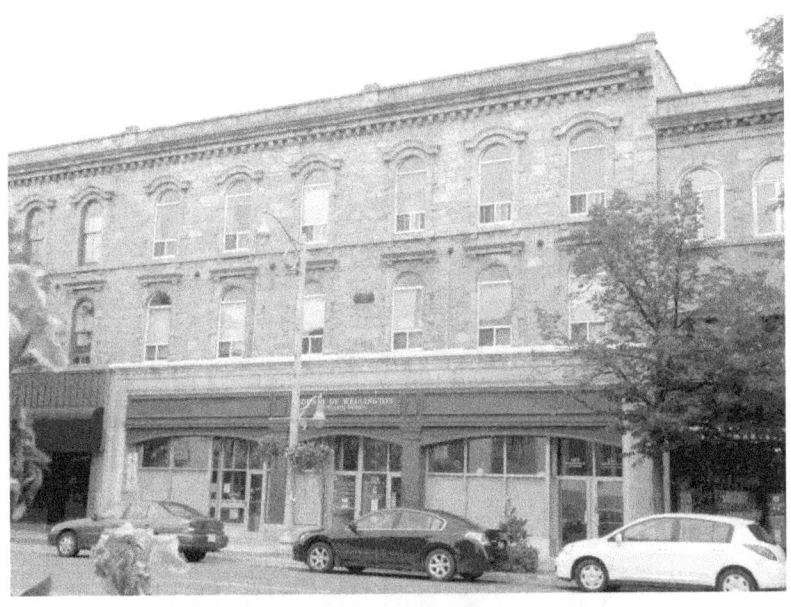

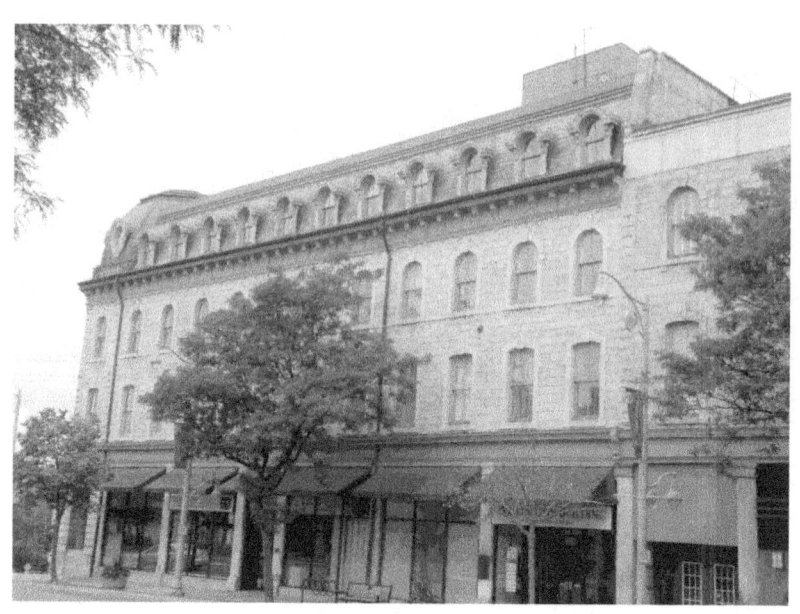

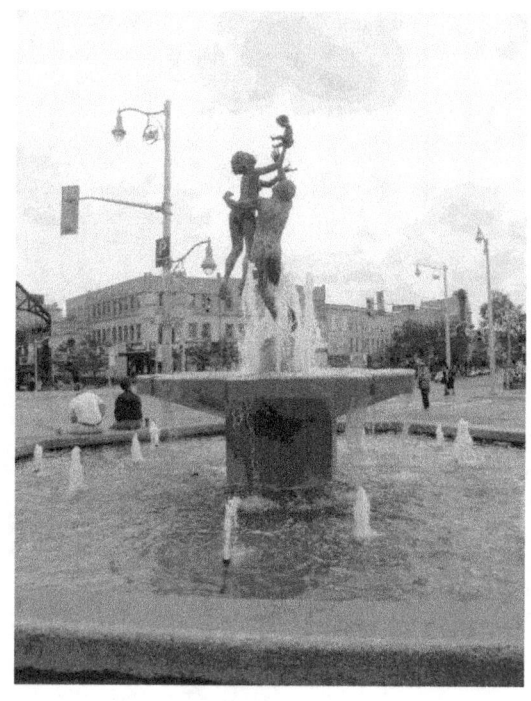

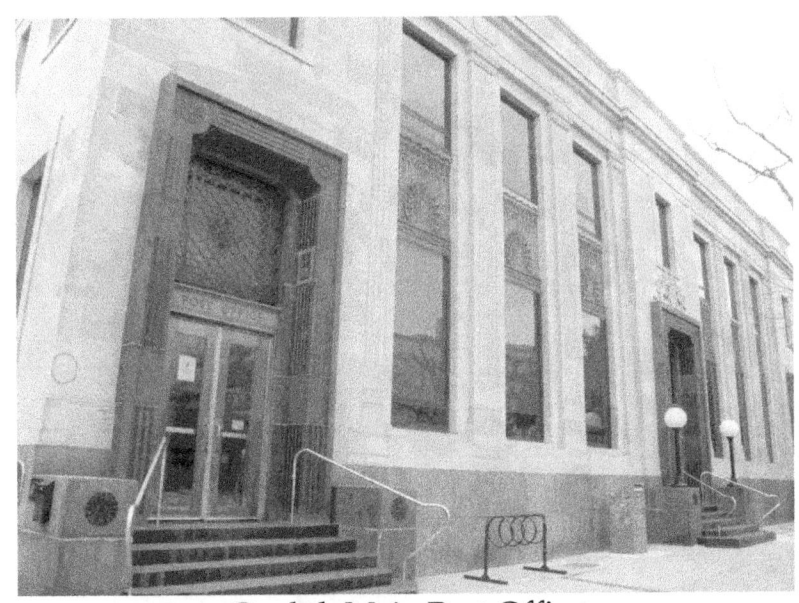

Guelph Main Post Office
74 Wyndham Street in Dominion Public Building

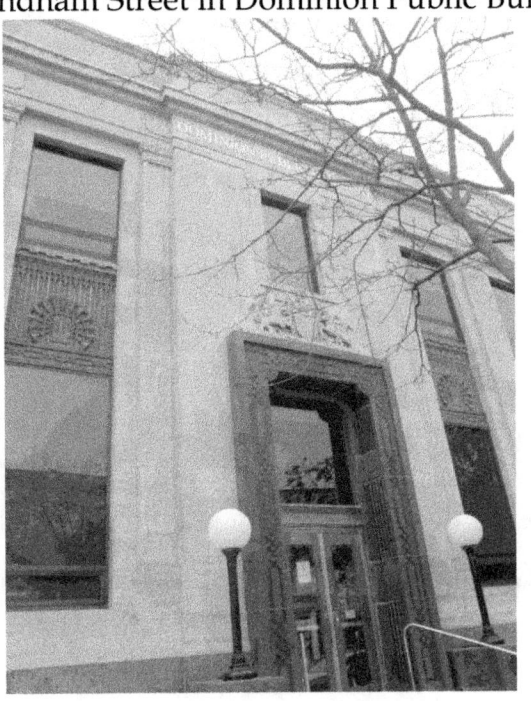

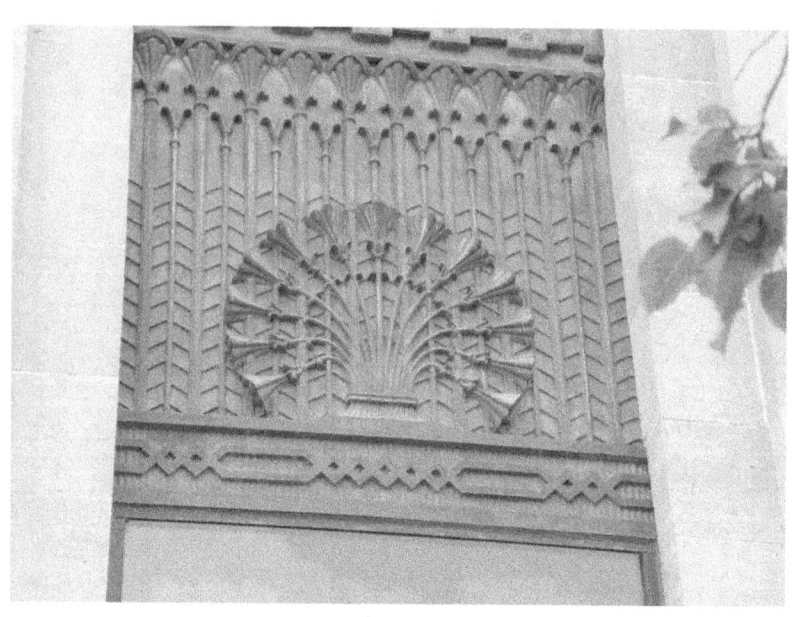

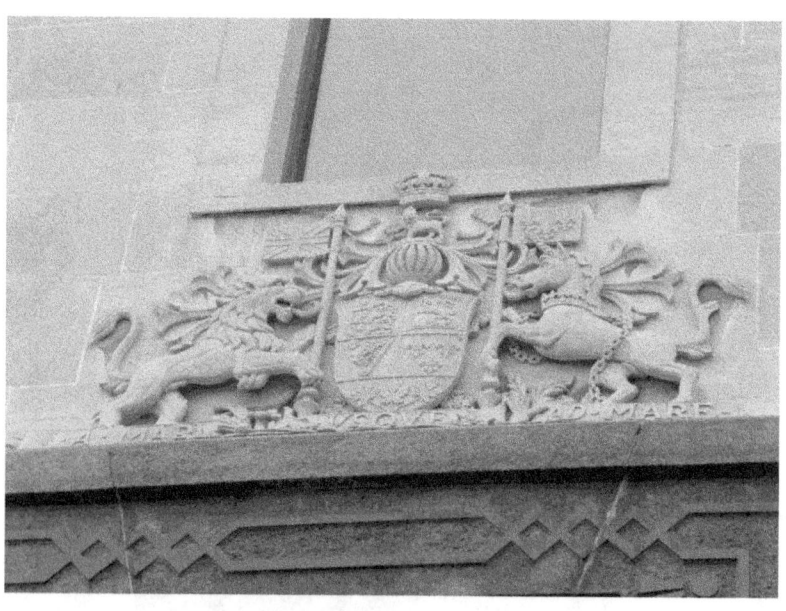

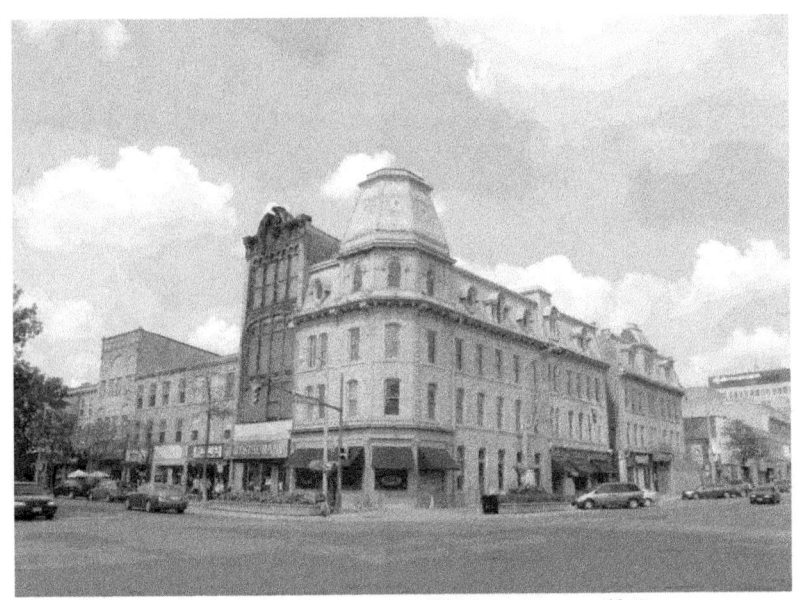

Corner of Wyndham and MacDonnell Streets

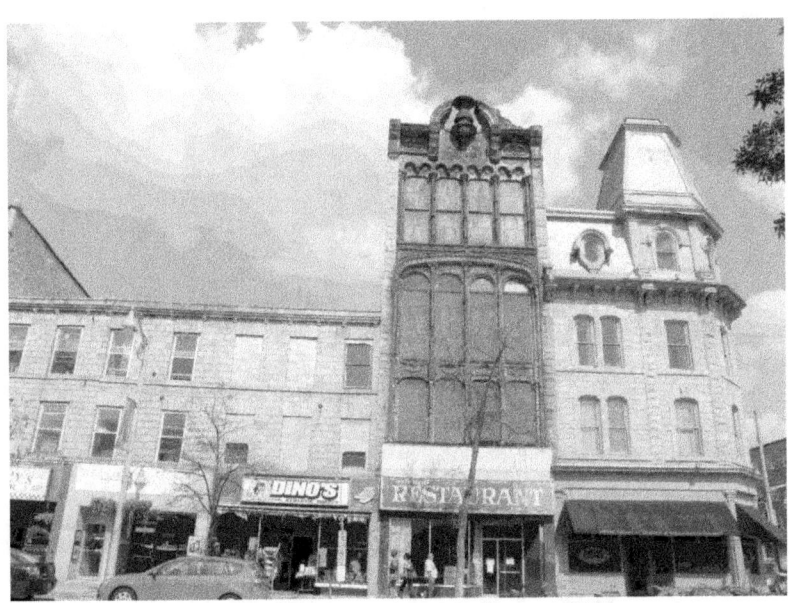

A. B. Petrie Building 1882

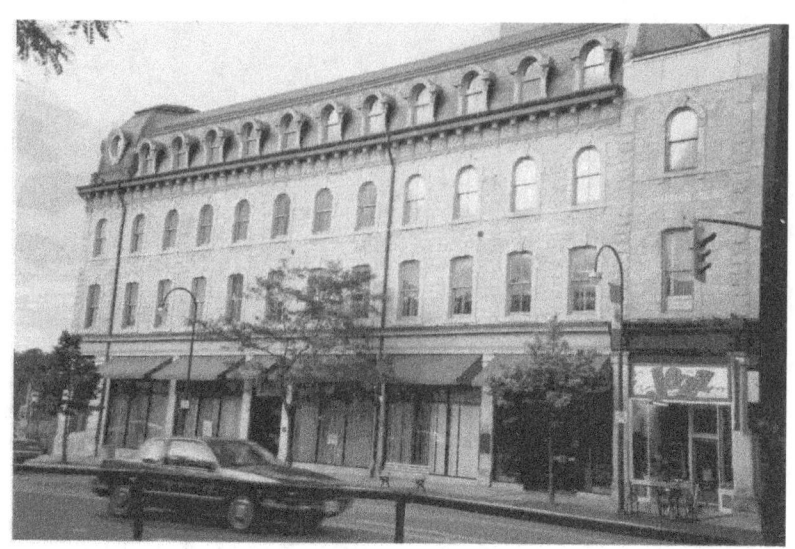

Guelph architecture

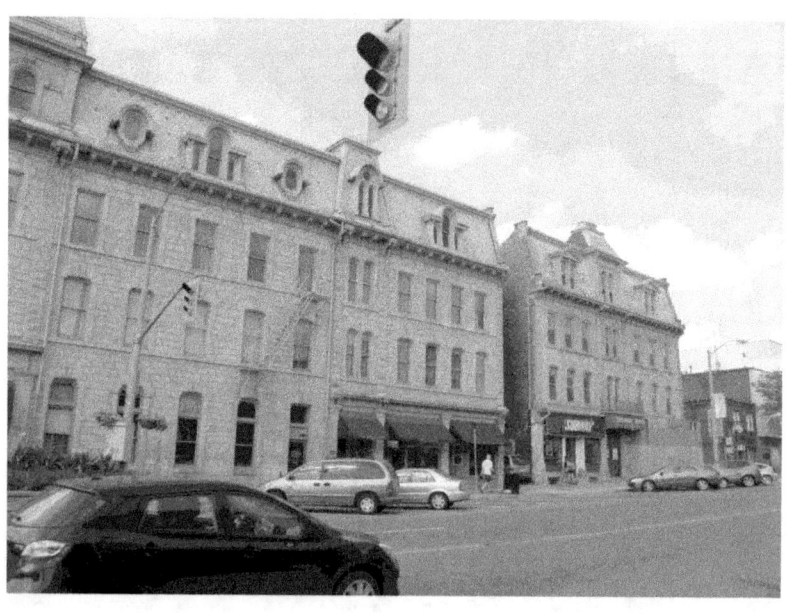

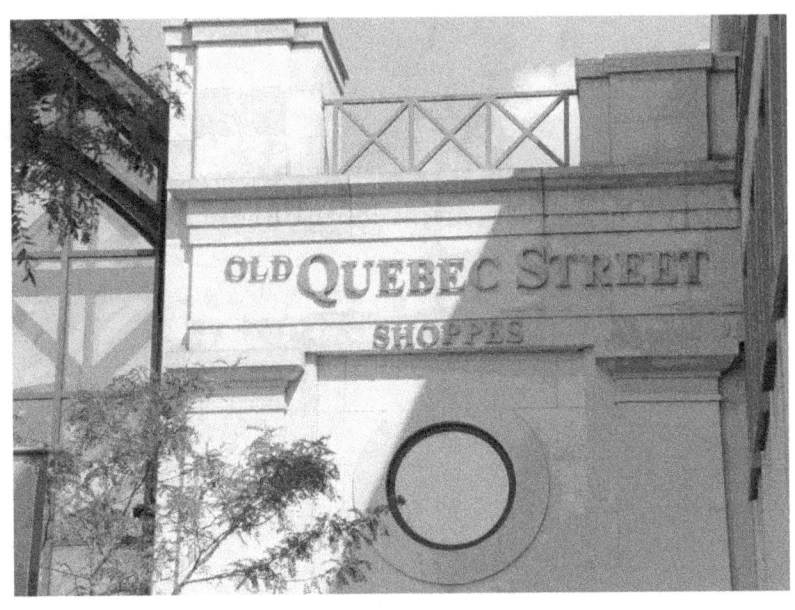

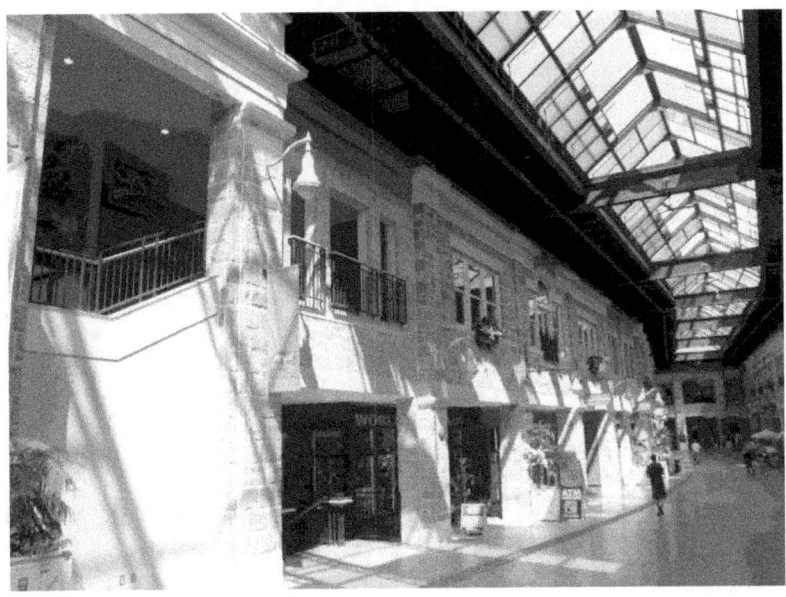

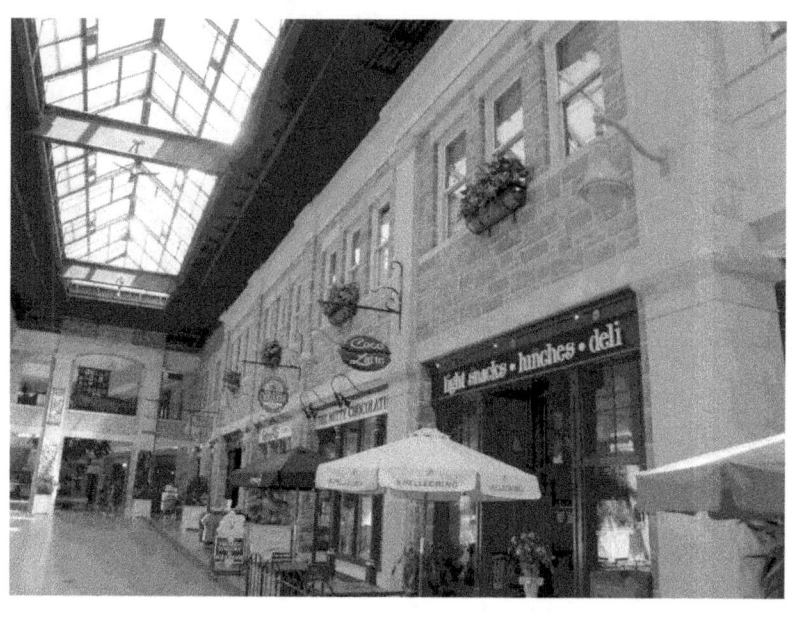

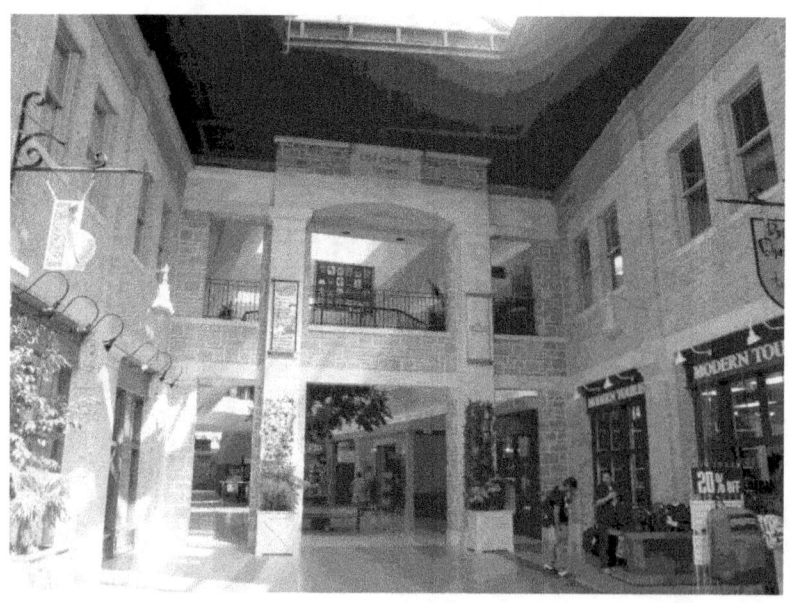

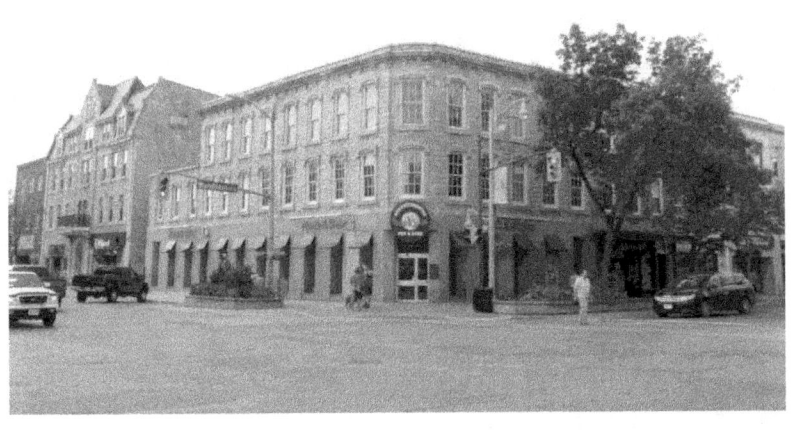

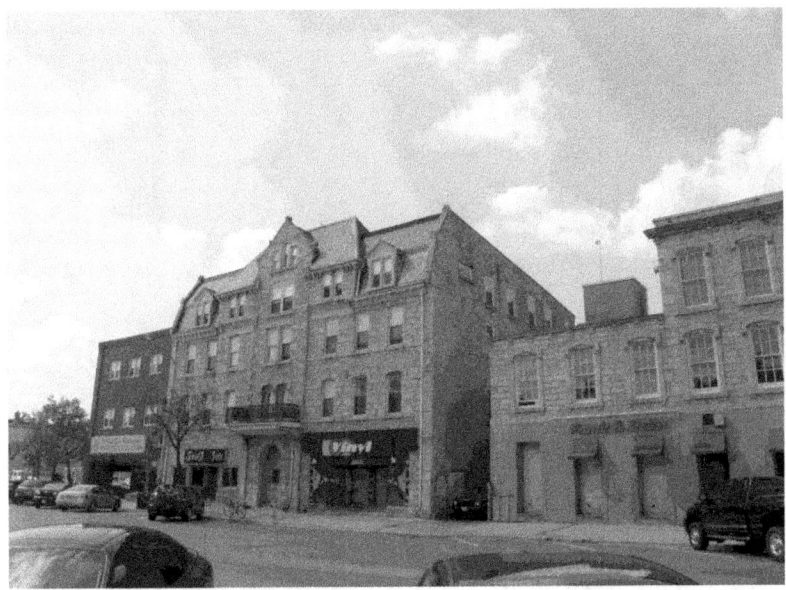

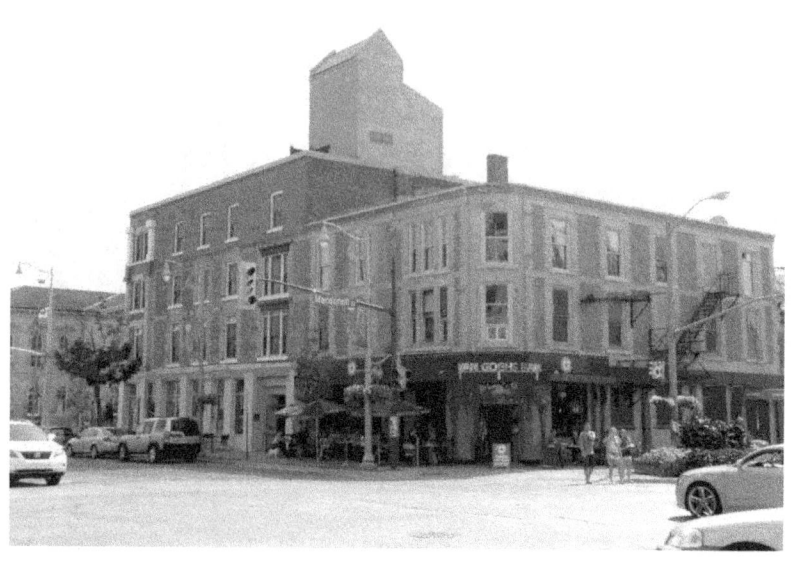

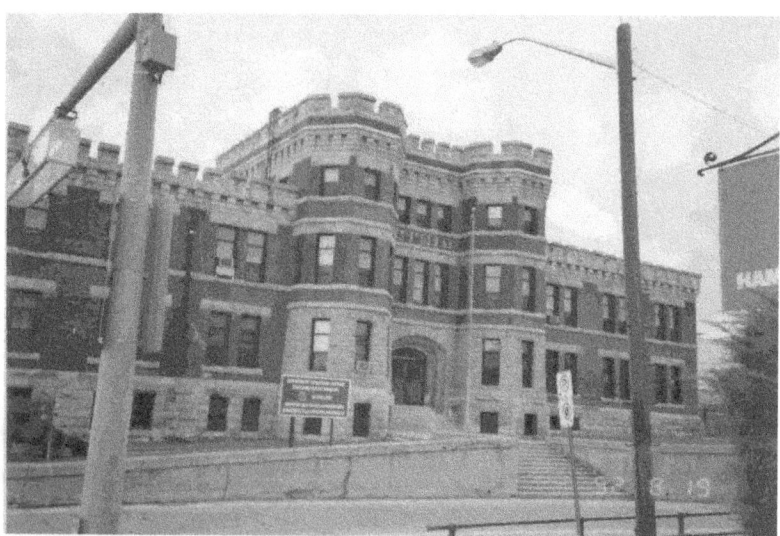

The Armoury – 7 Wyndham Street South

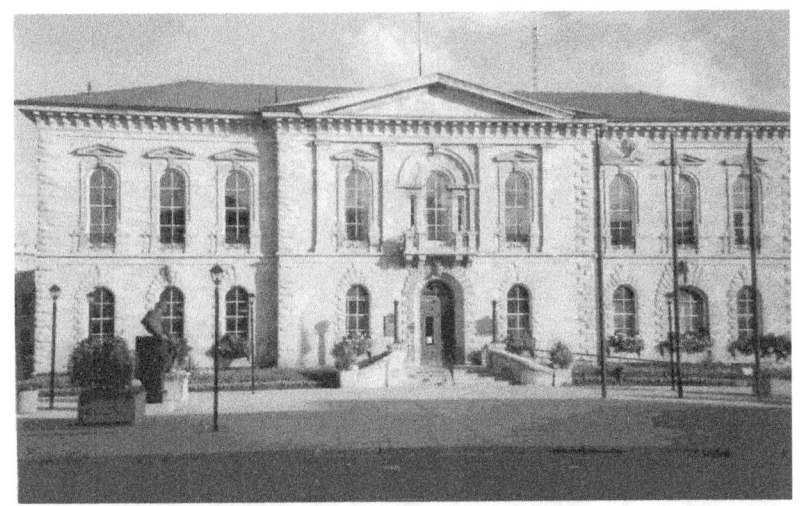

Guelph City Hall – 1 Carden Street

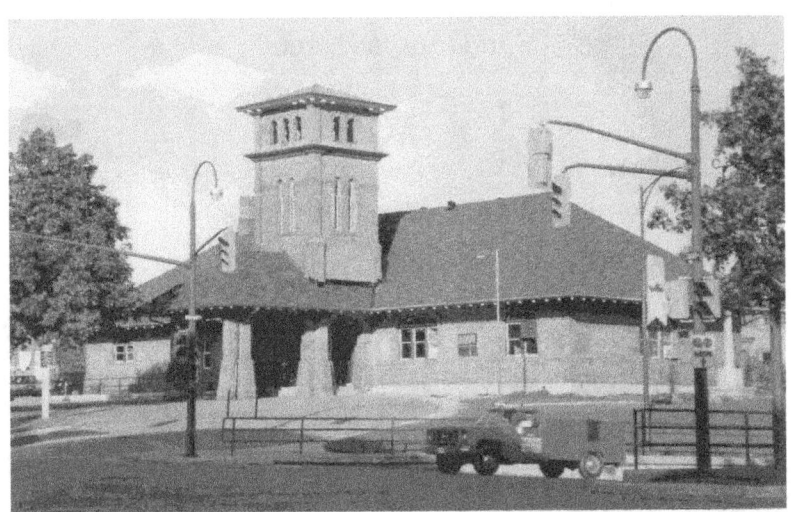

Guelph Train Station on Carden Street

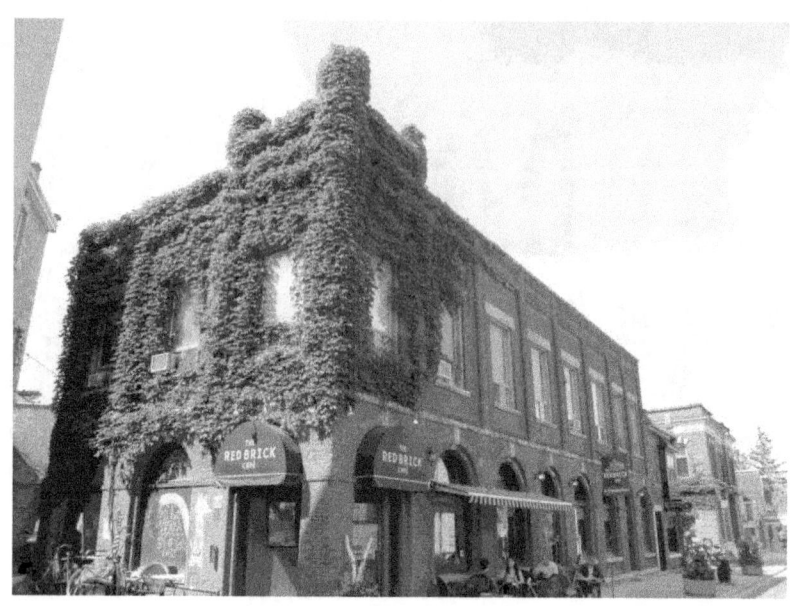

On Douglas Street

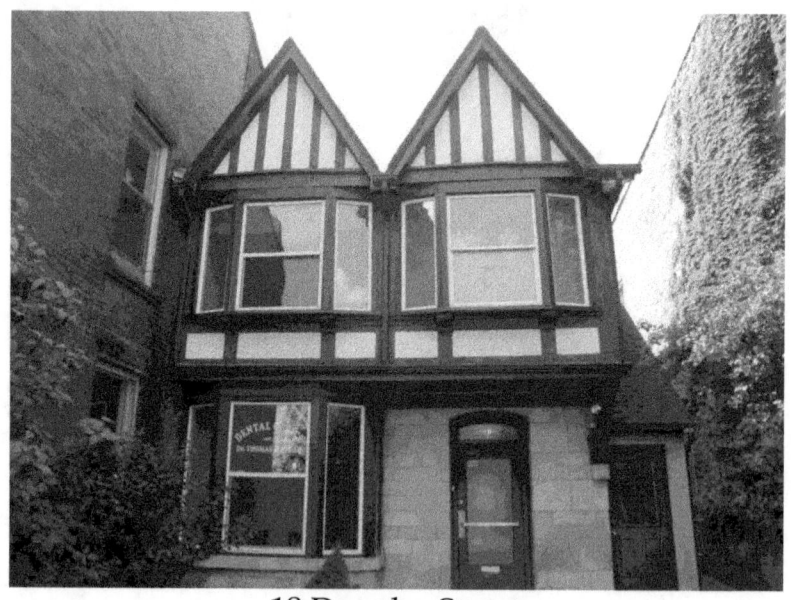

18 Douglas Street

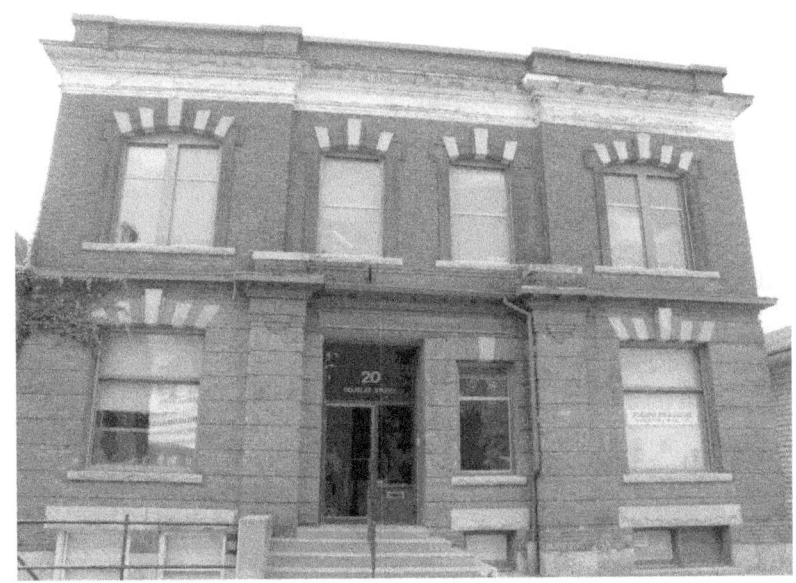

20 Douglas Street

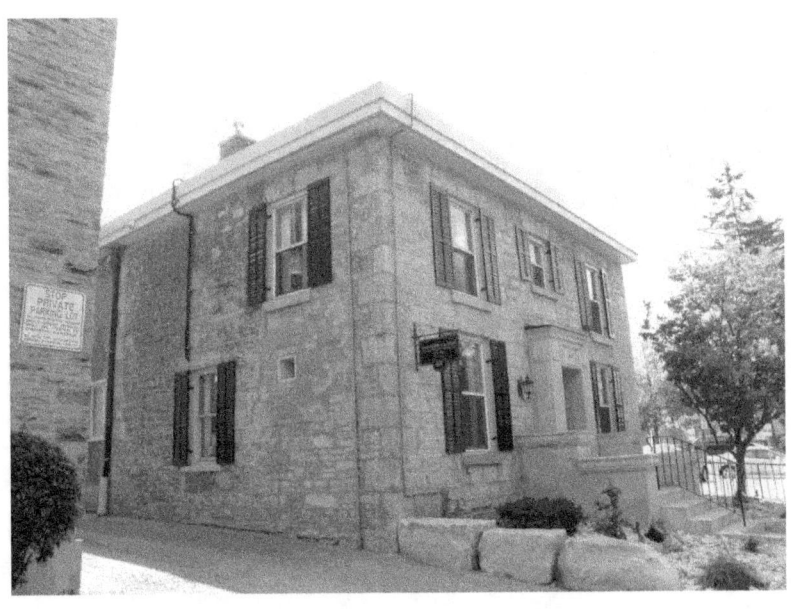

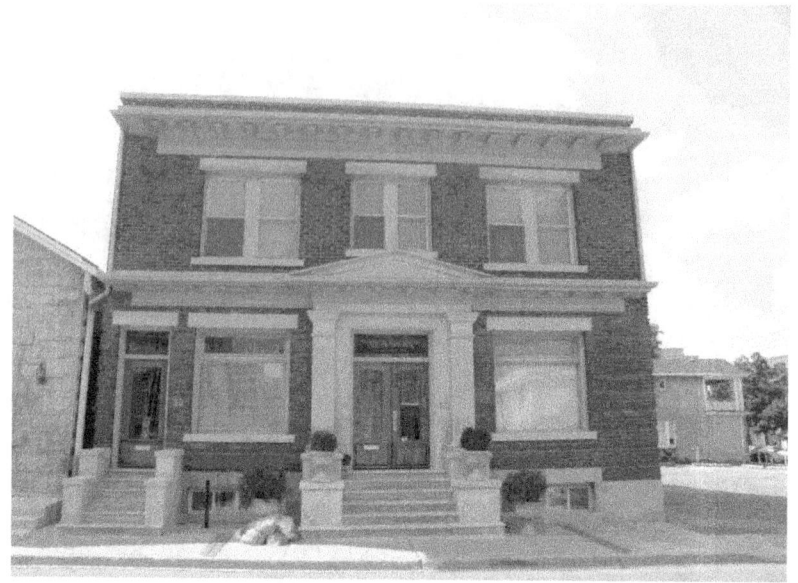

30 Douglas Street

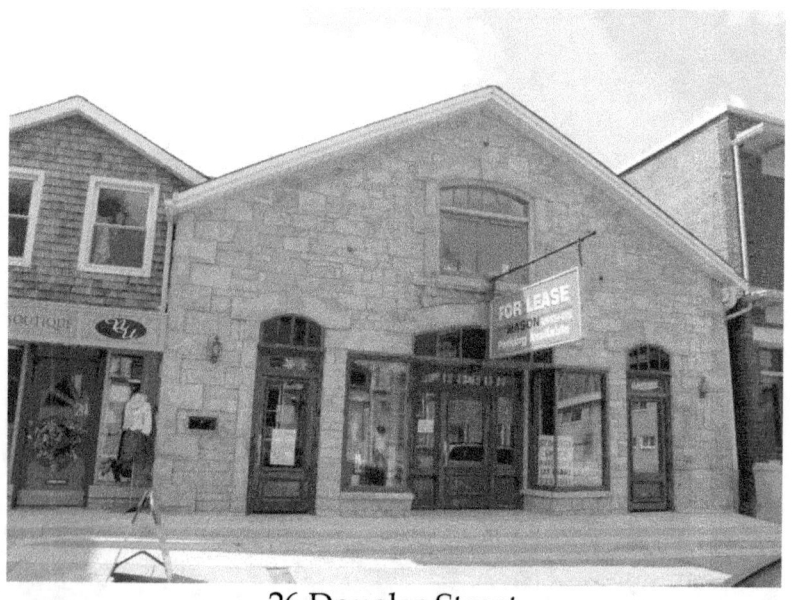

26 Douglas Street

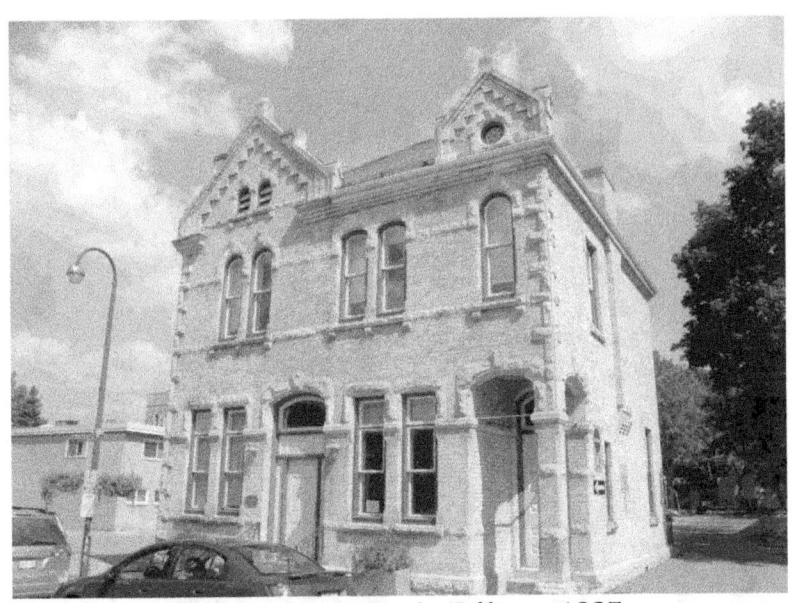

Crown Attorney's Office - 1885
Douglas Street

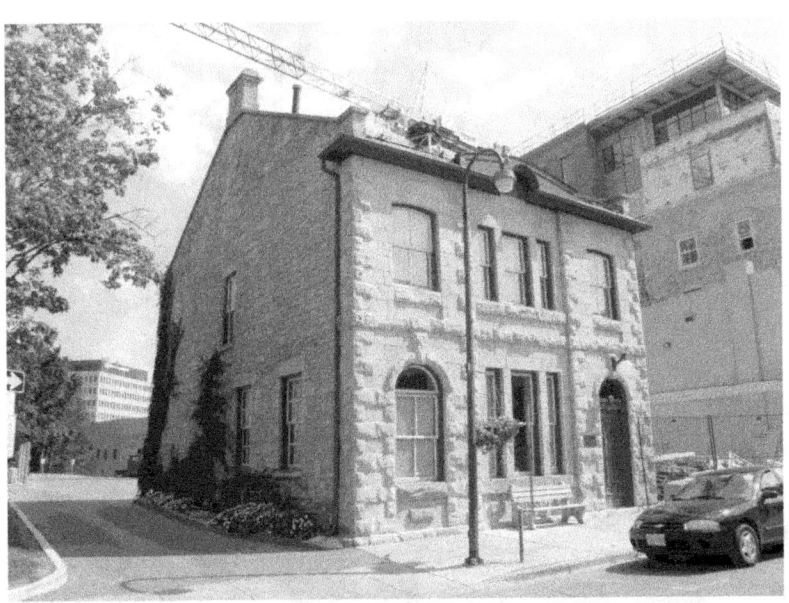

County Solicitor's Building – 1863-65
15 Douglas Street

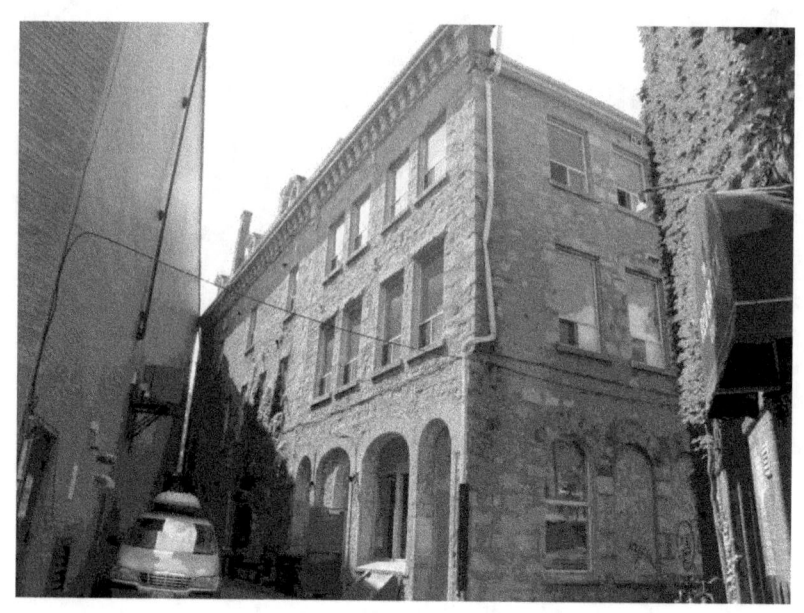

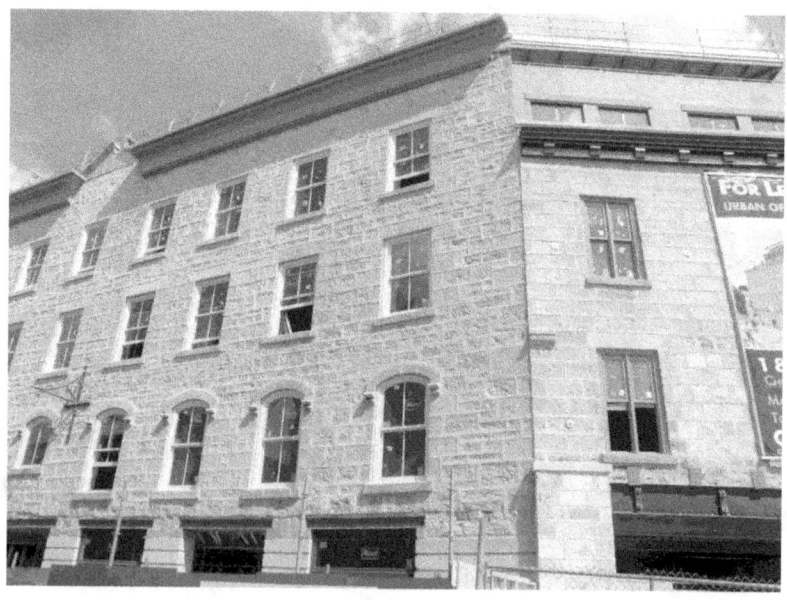

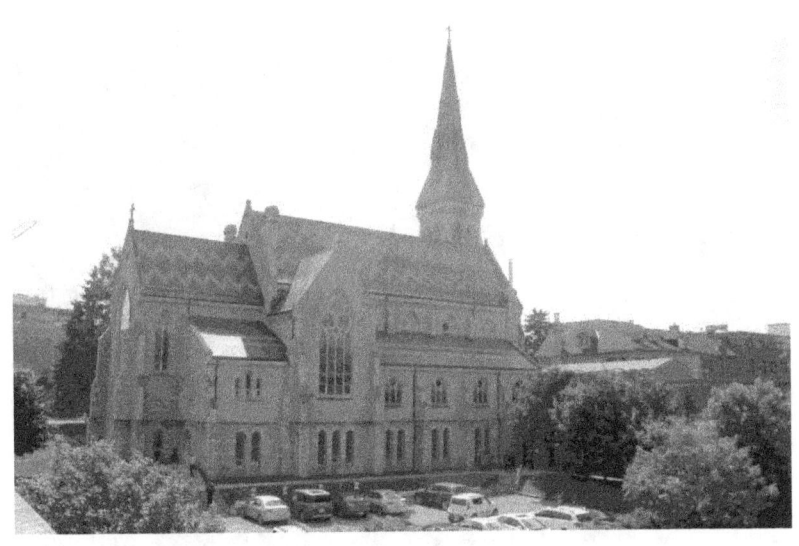

Saint George's Anglican Church - 1857
99 Woolwich Street

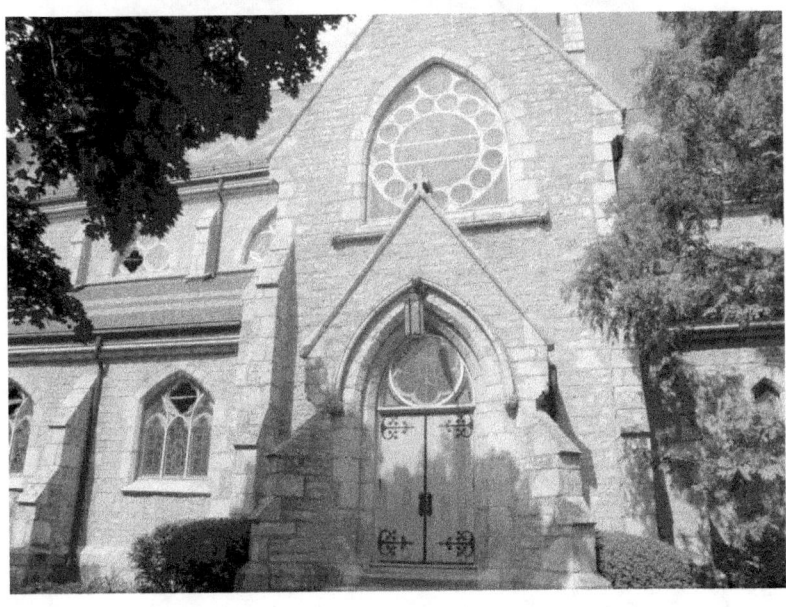

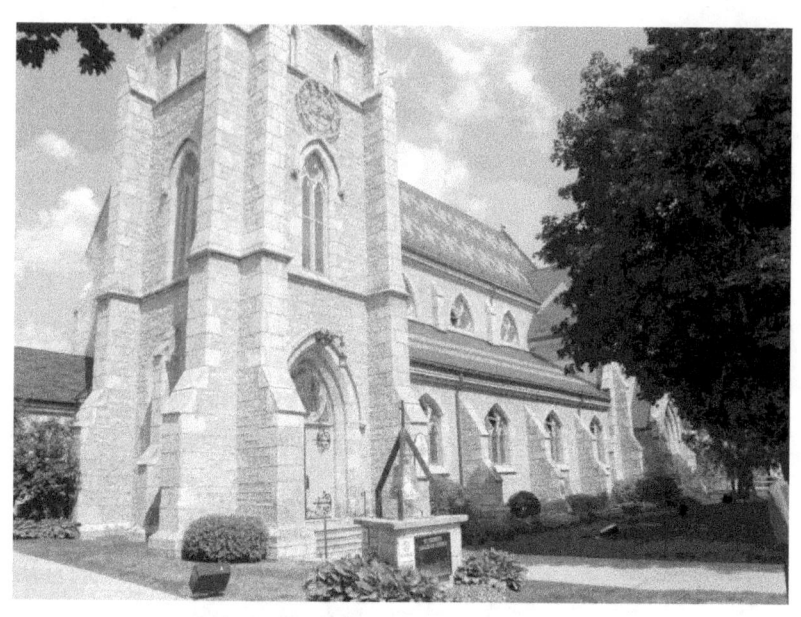

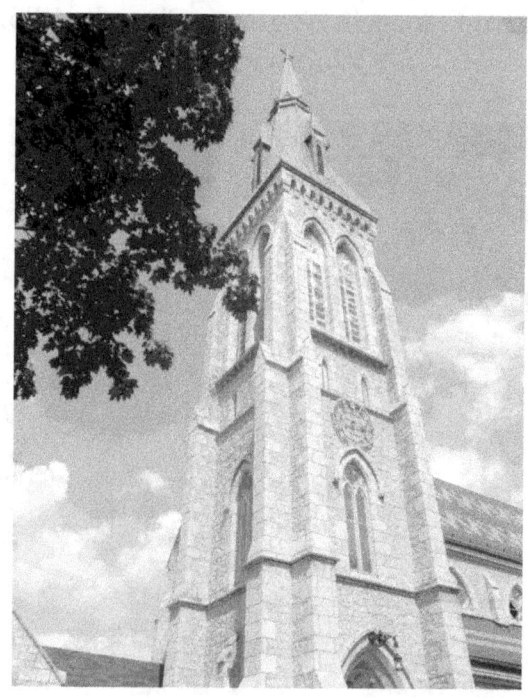

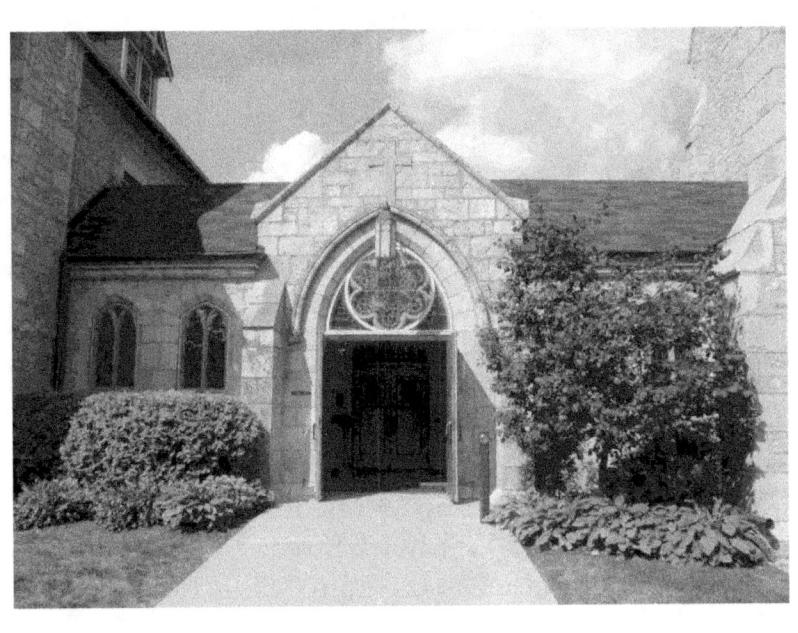

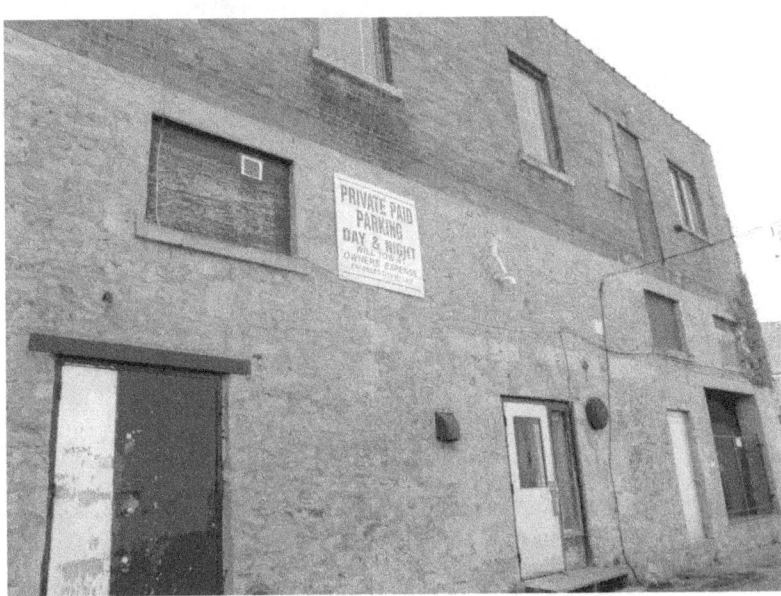

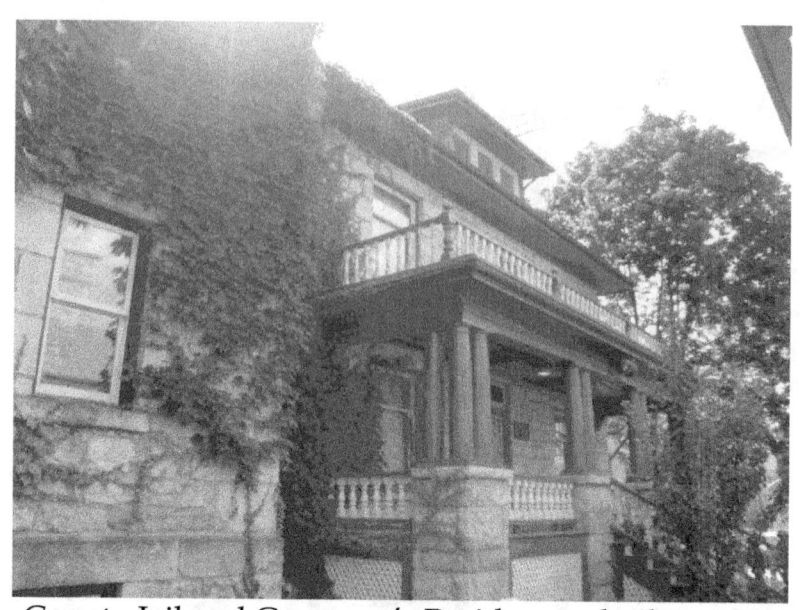

County Jail and Governor's Residence – built in 1911
74 Woolwich Street
Two-storey limestone in the Late Gothic Revival Style

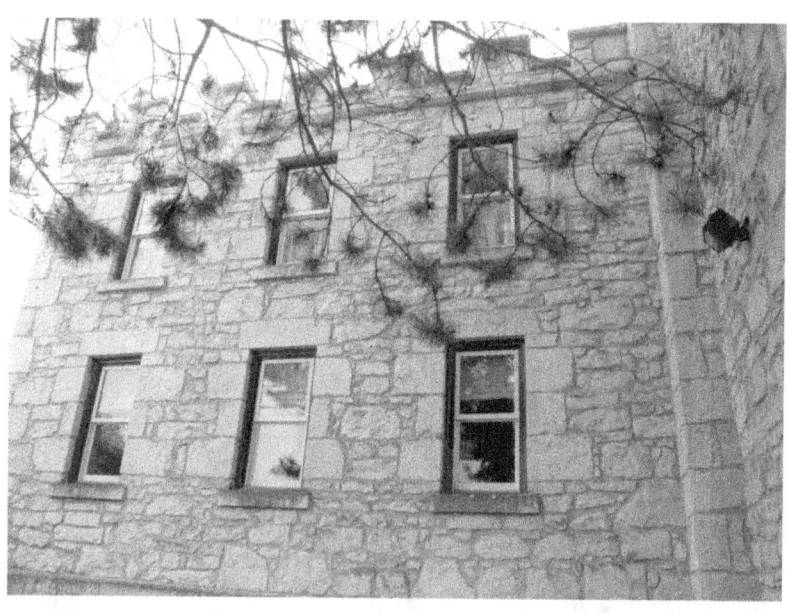

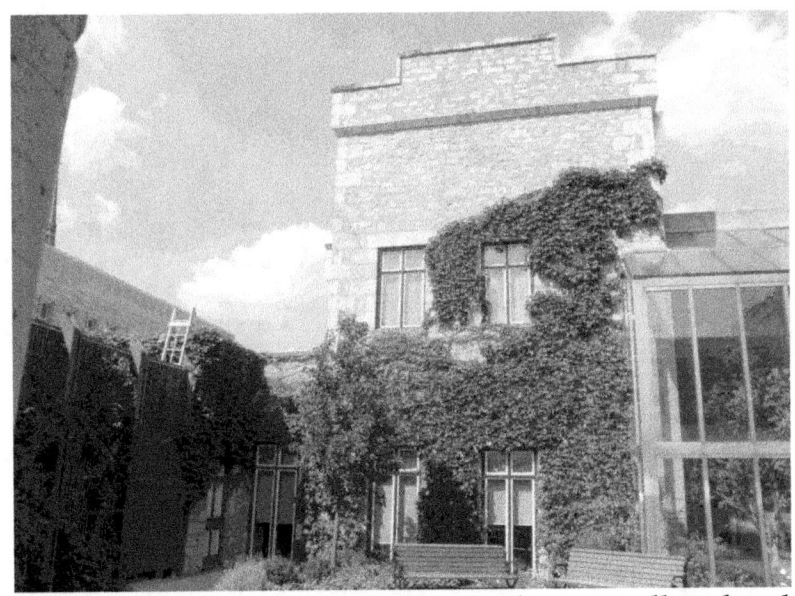

Wellington County Court house built in castellated style reminiscent of medieval fortifications, erected in 1842-44 and expanded many times, each addition complementing the design of the original structure.
Now Wellington County Administration Centre

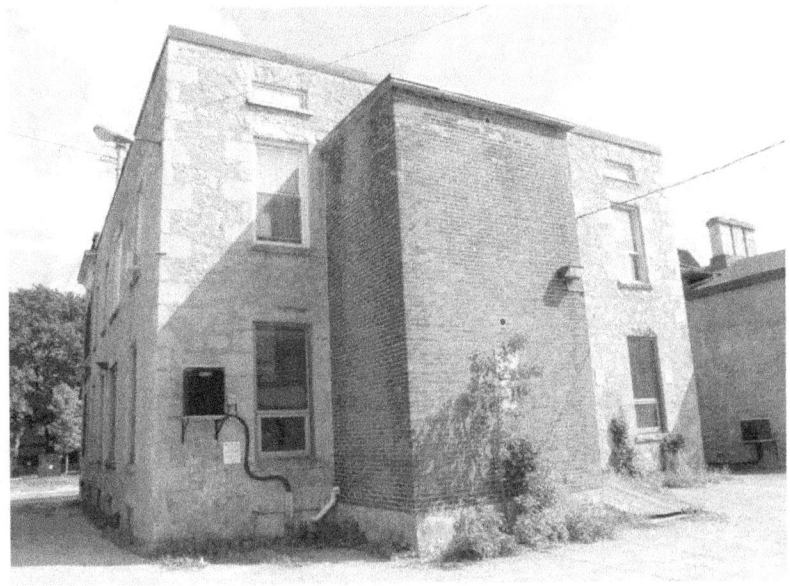

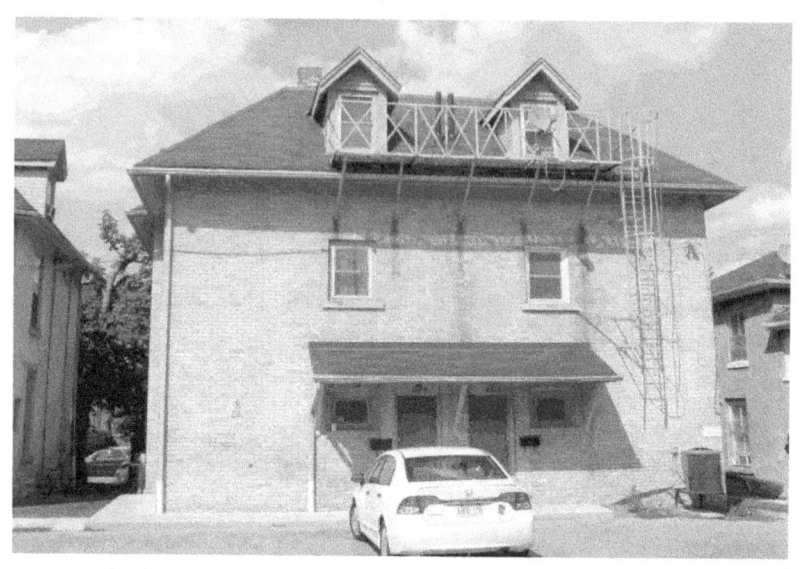

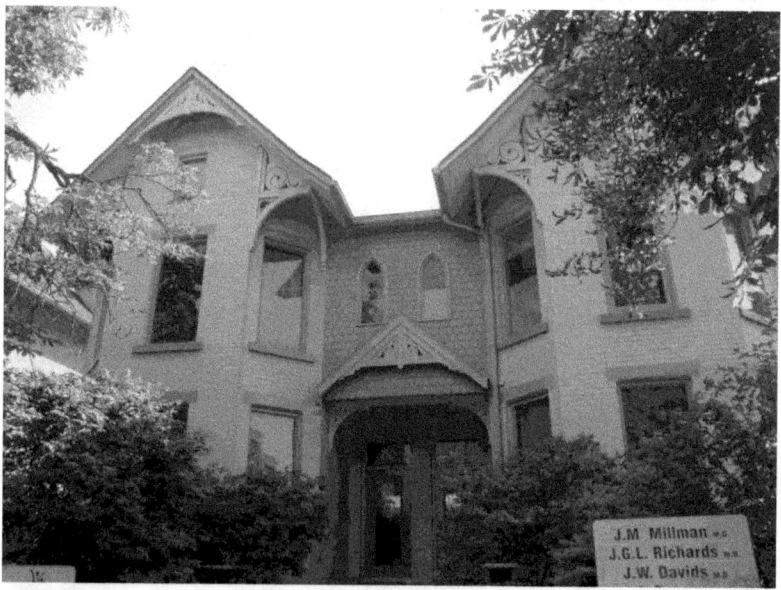

#110

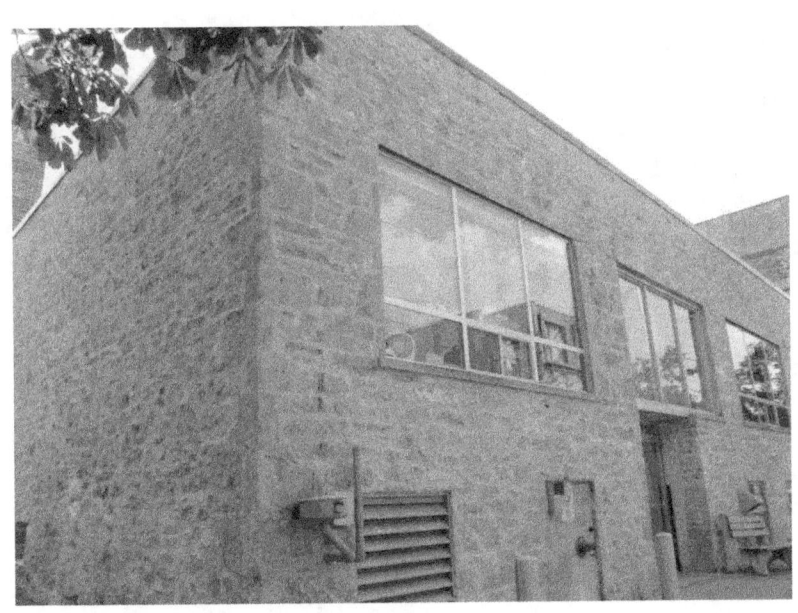

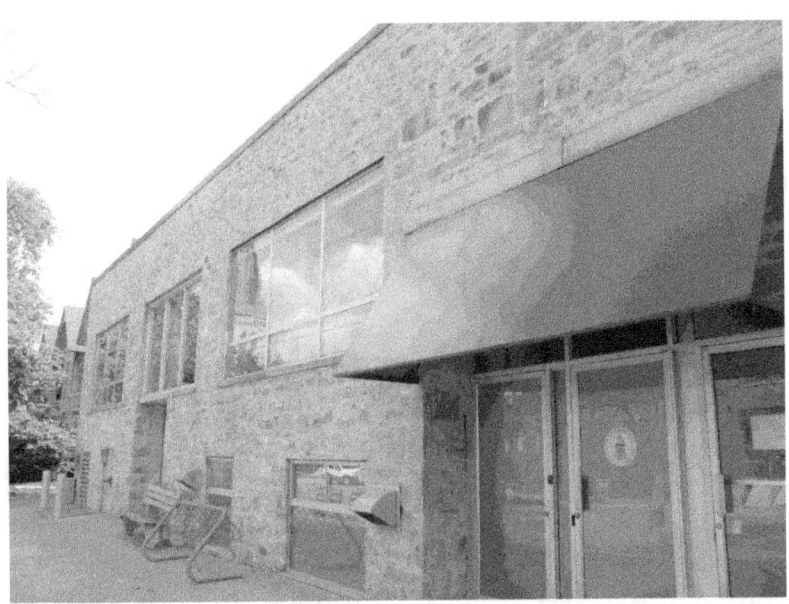

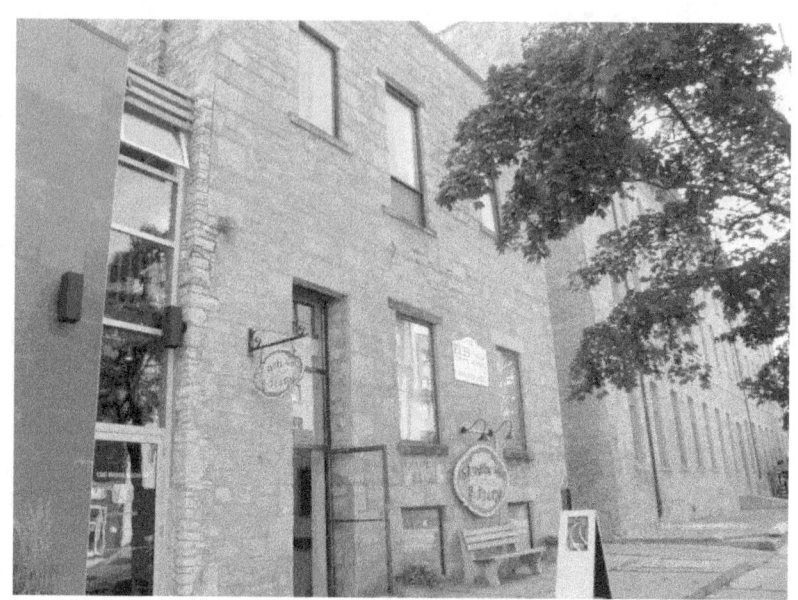

#128

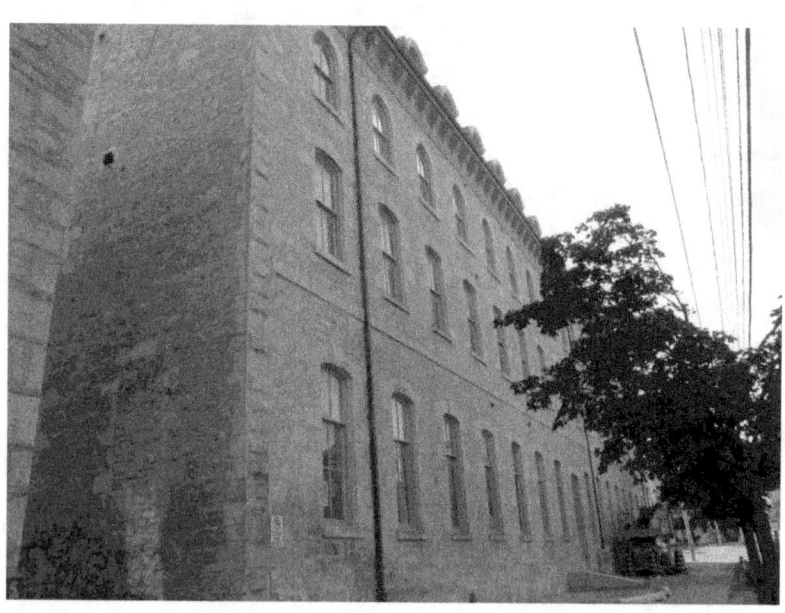

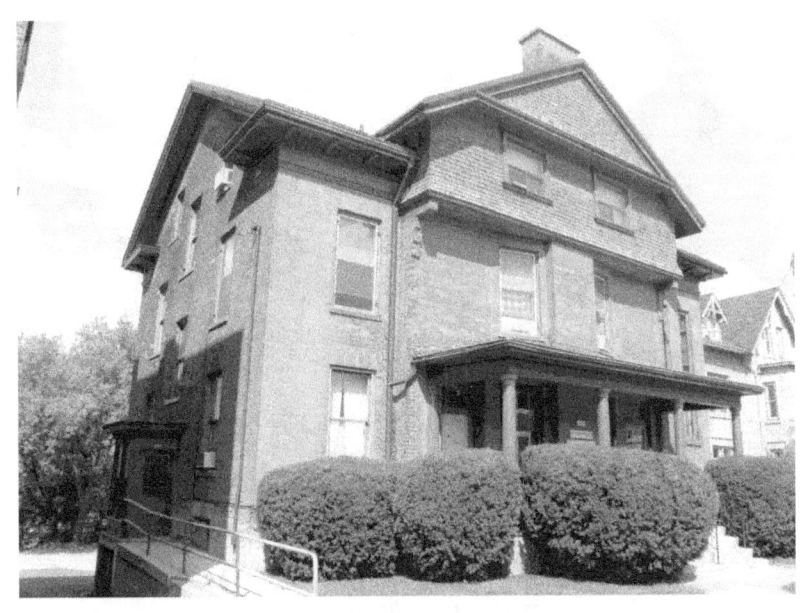

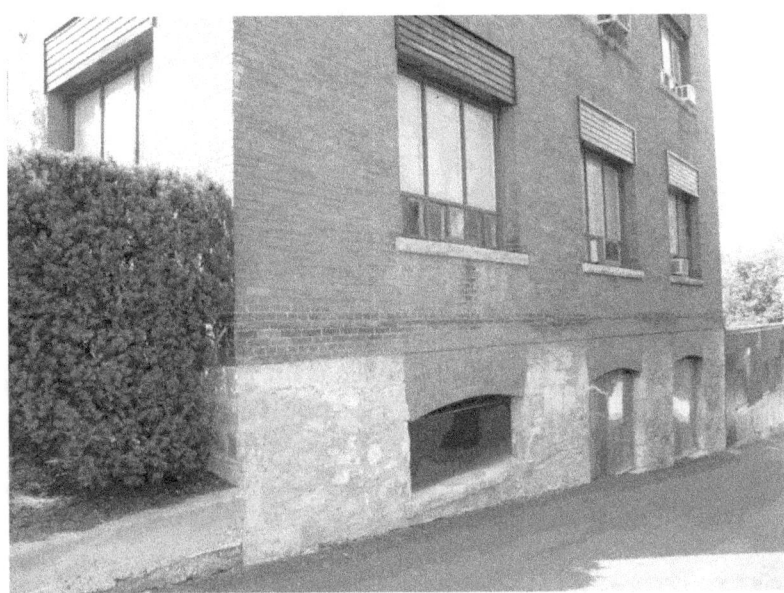

Old stone foundation

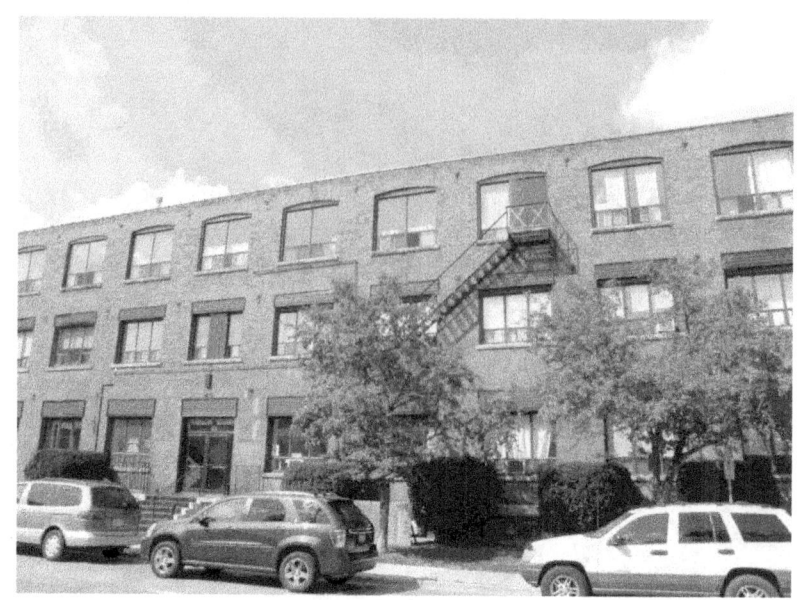

Trafalgar Building
#123

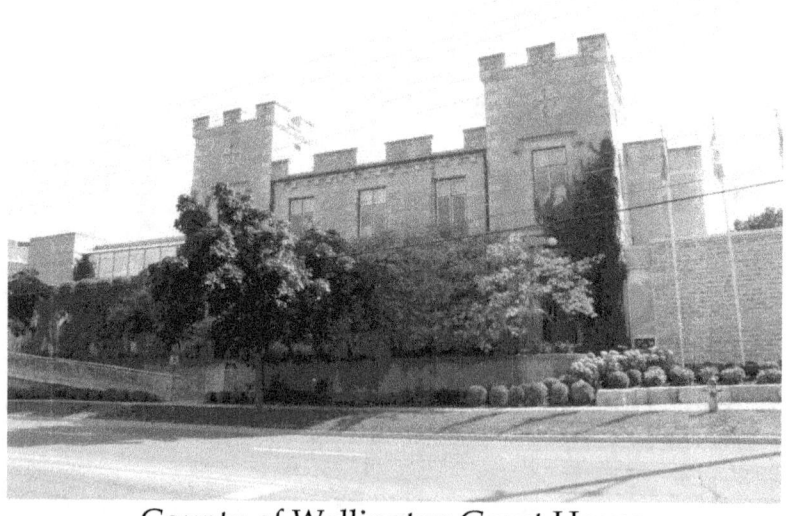

County of Wellington Court House
74 Woolwich Street

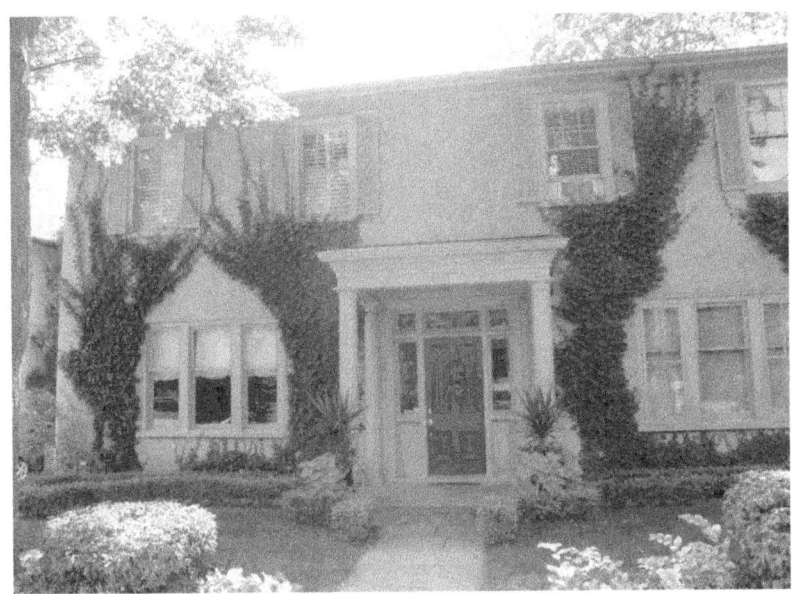

68 Arthur Street North

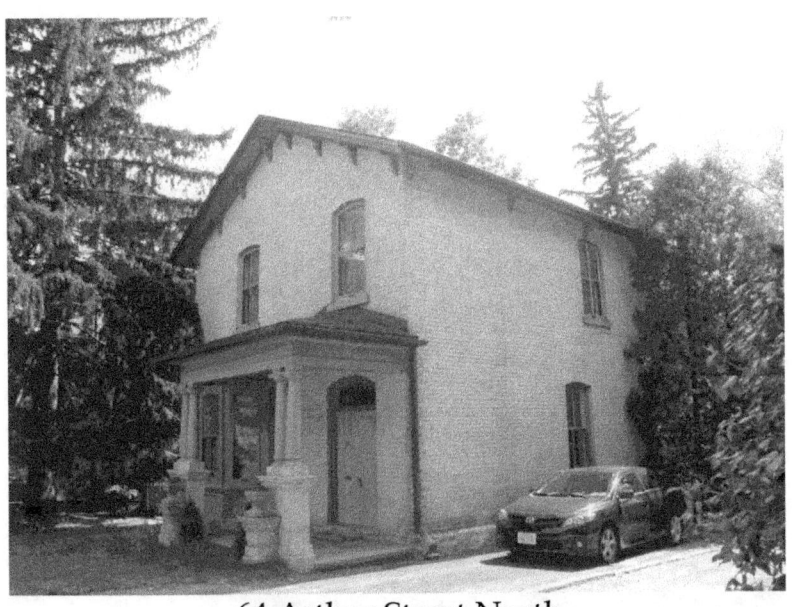

64 Arthur Street North
Single cornice brackets

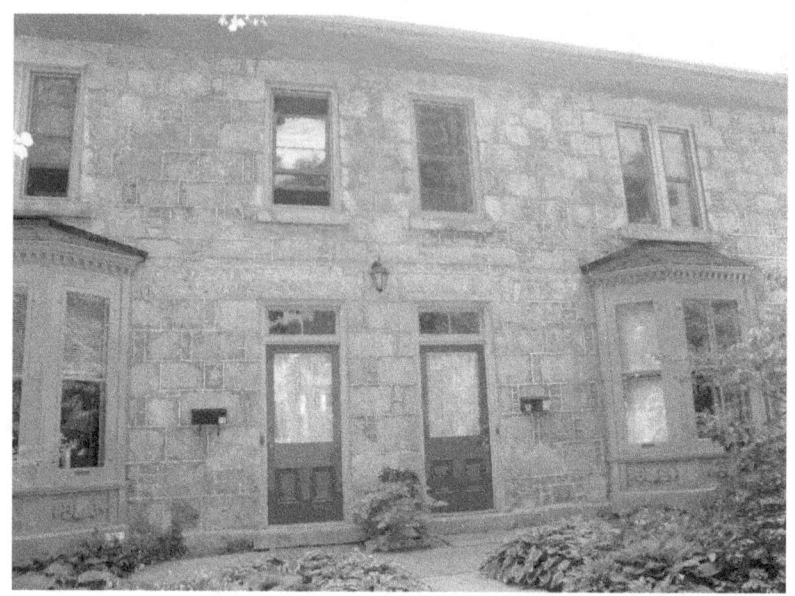

50/52 Arthur Street North

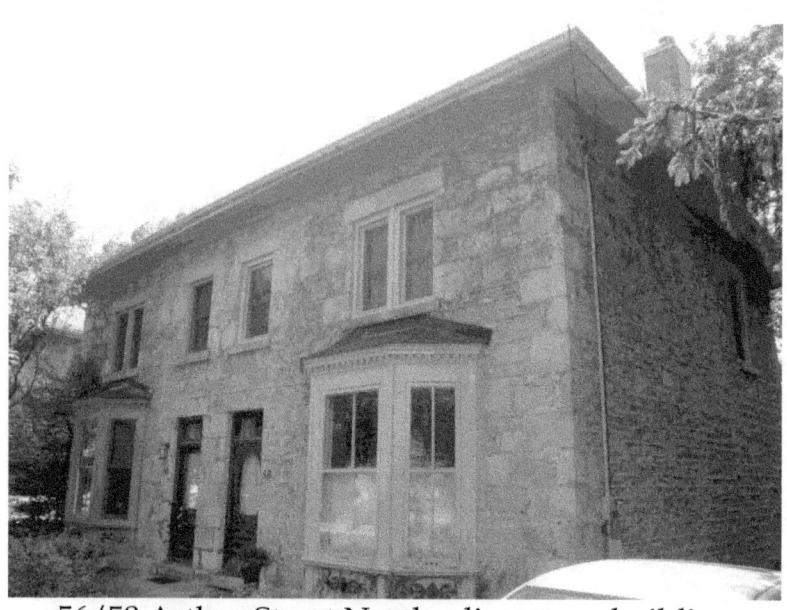

56/58 Arthur Street North – limestone building

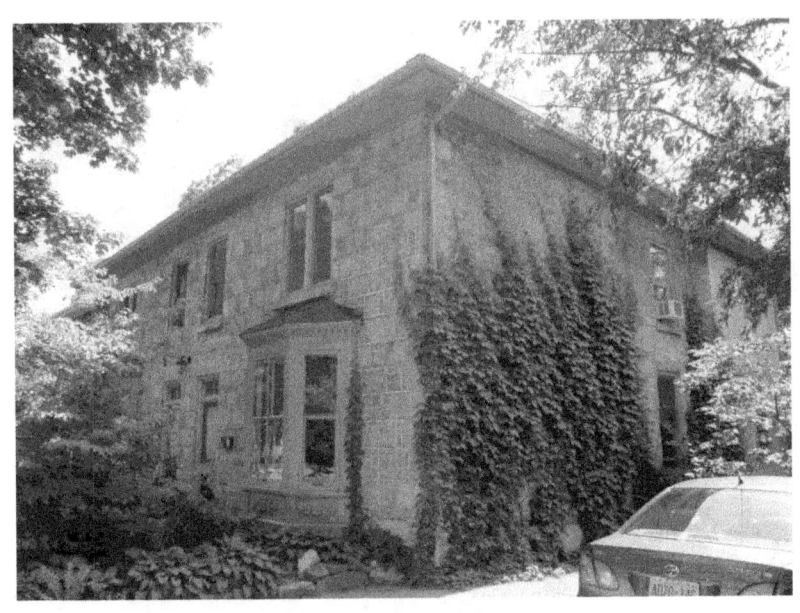

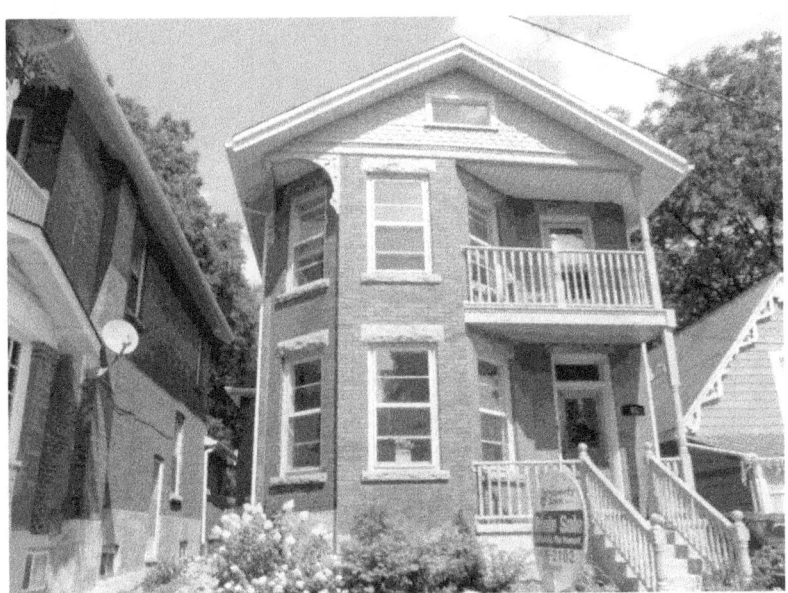

45 Arthur Street North

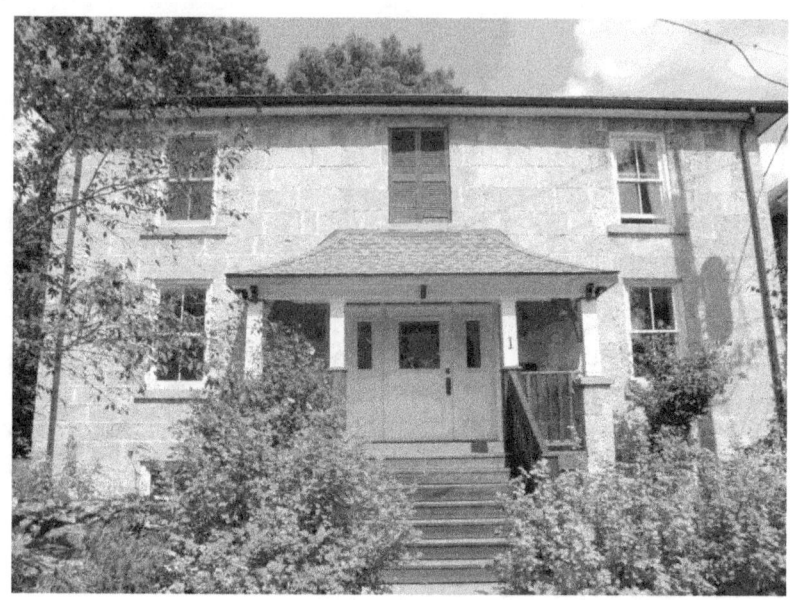

1 Queen Street

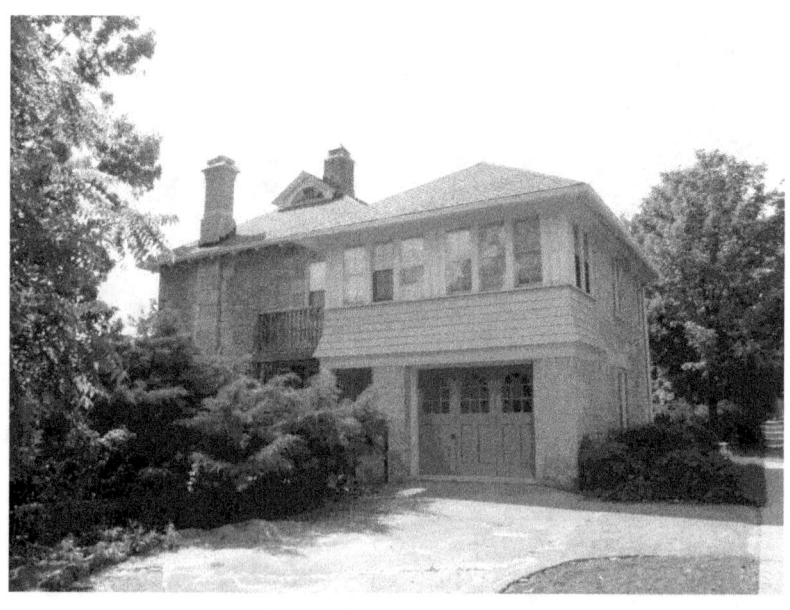

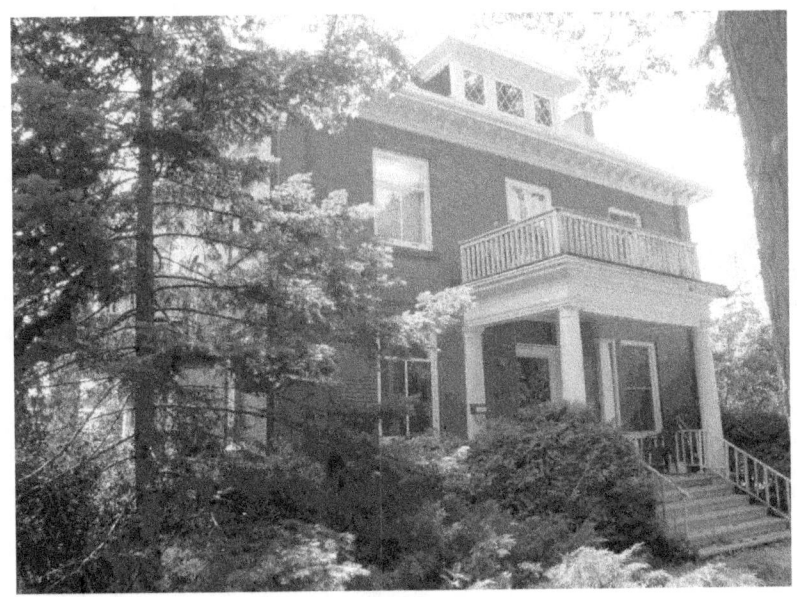

#92

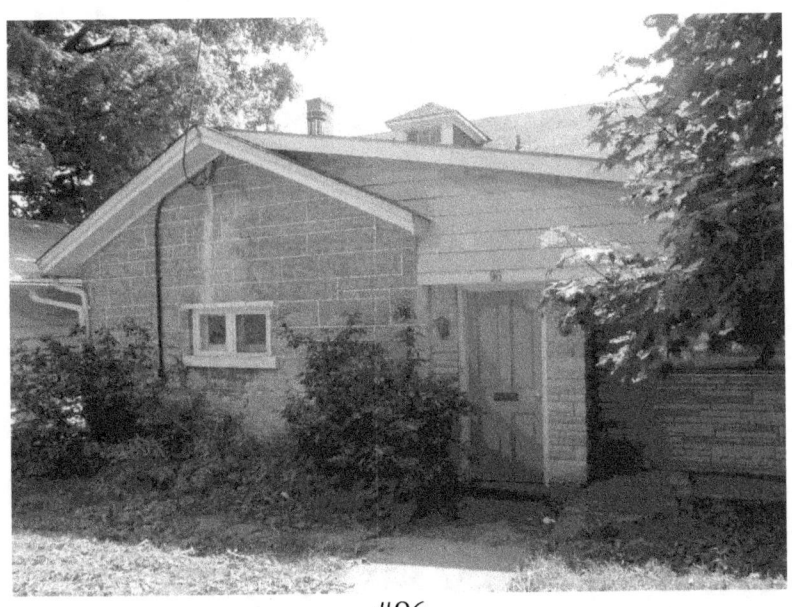

#96

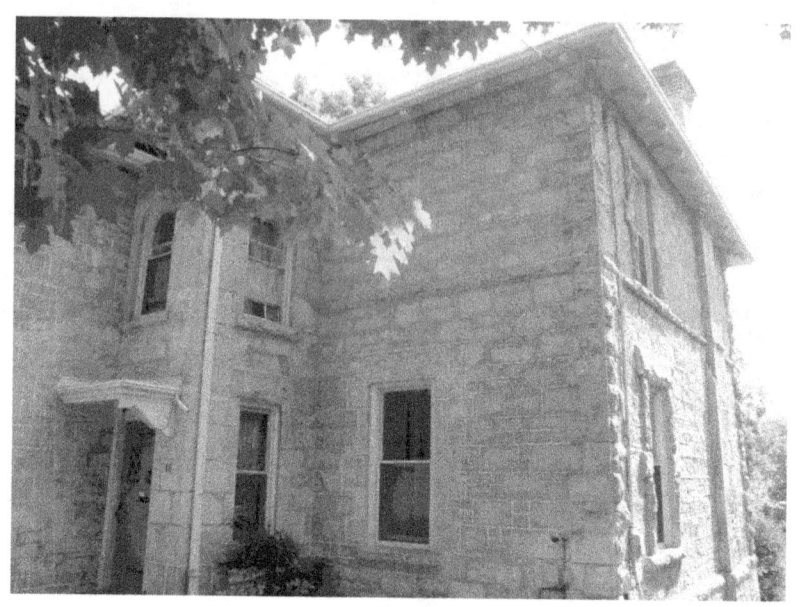

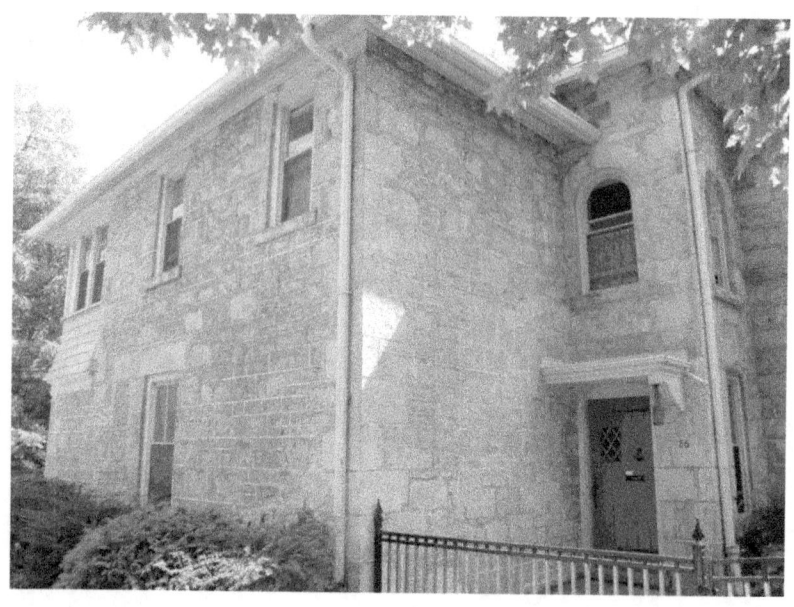

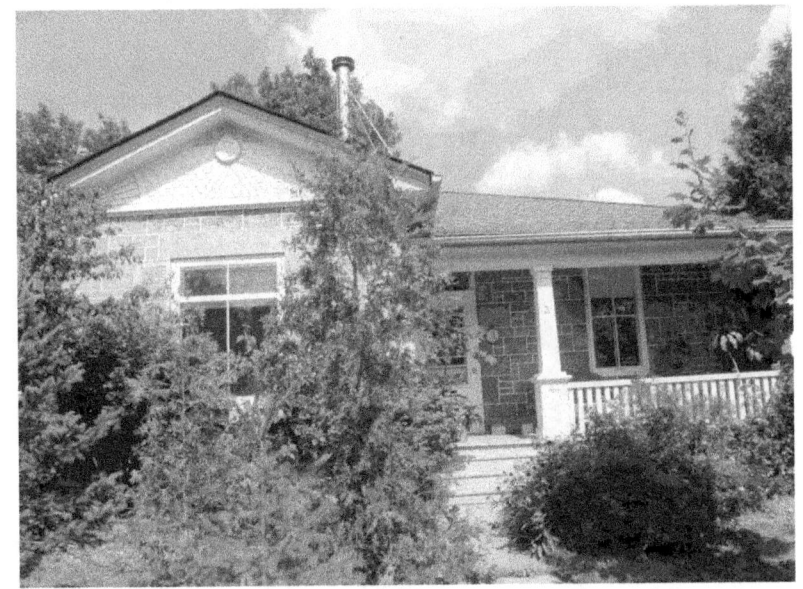

#3

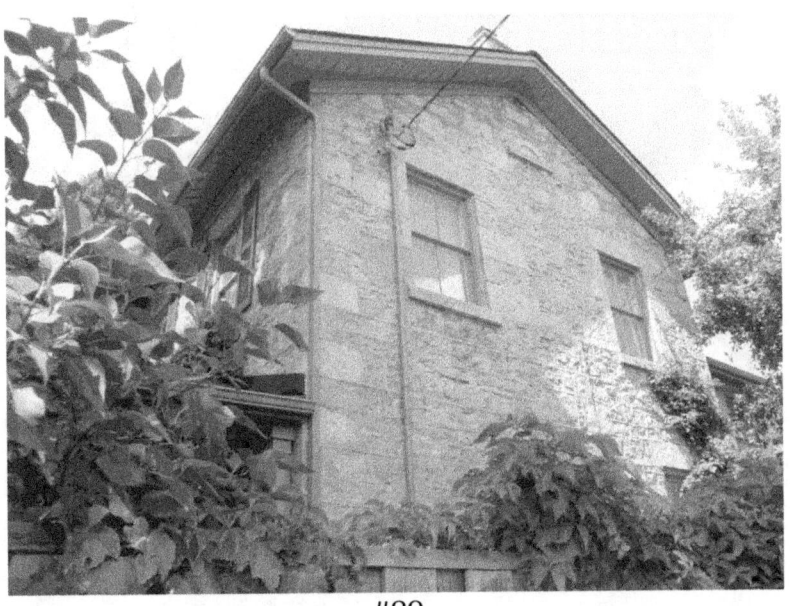

#89

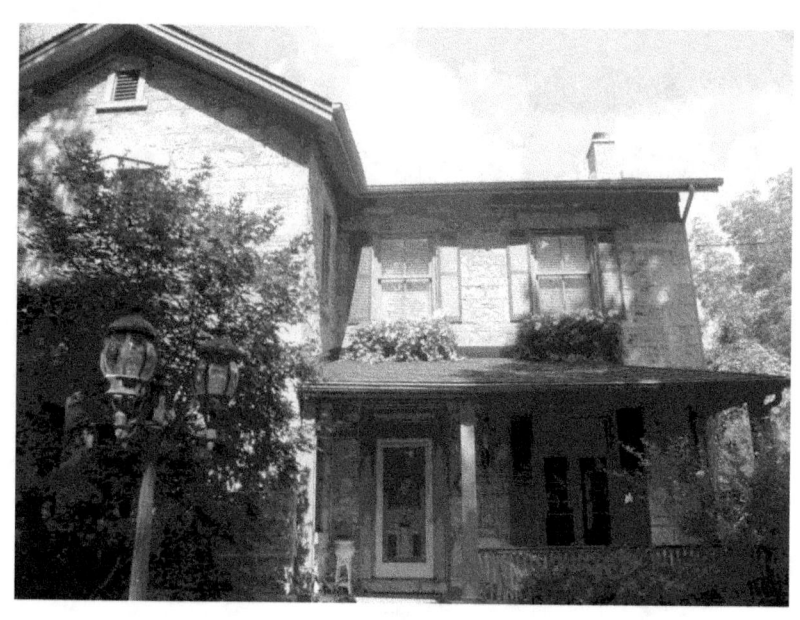

#89

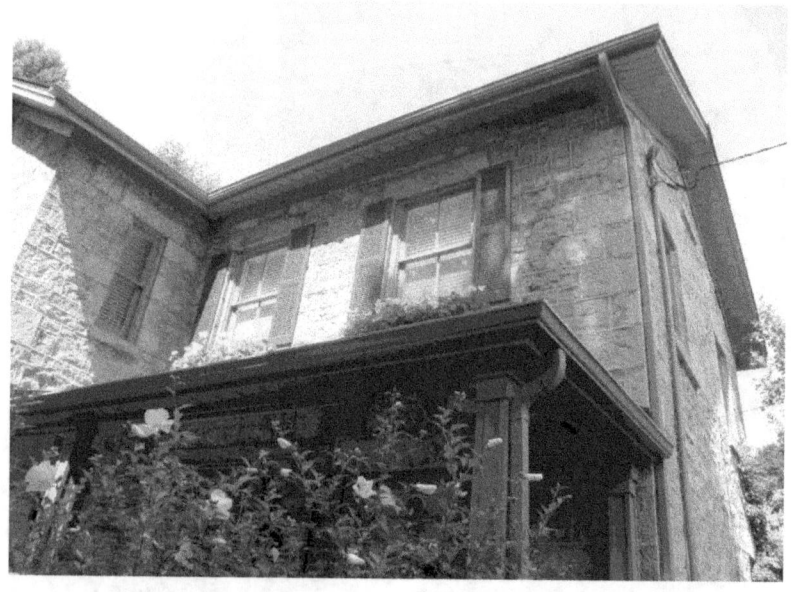

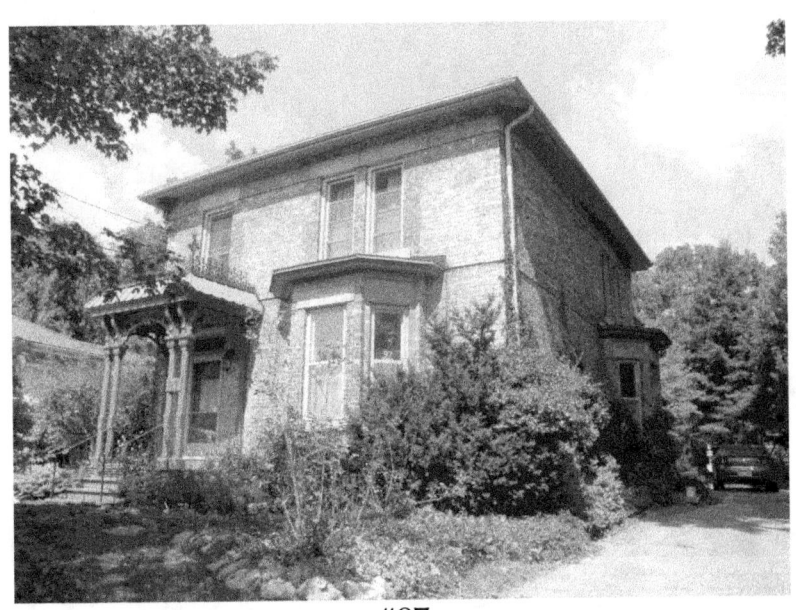

#97

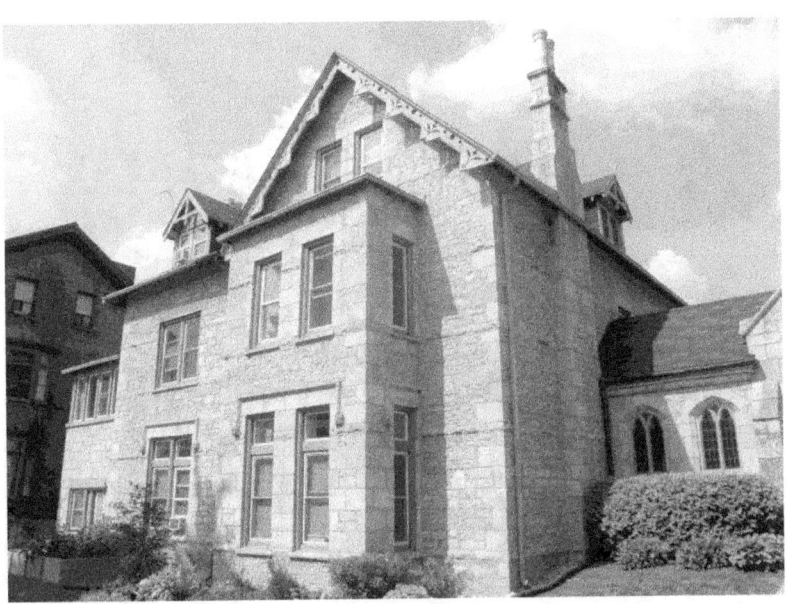

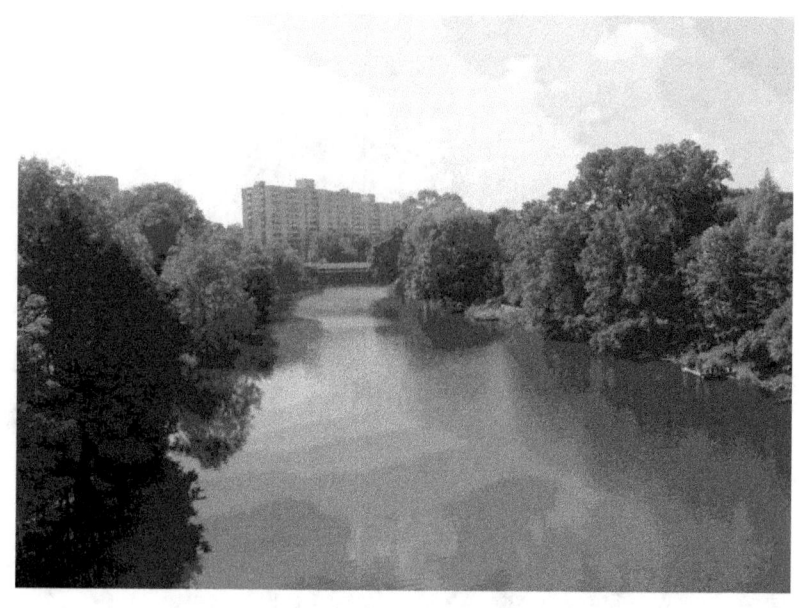

River views

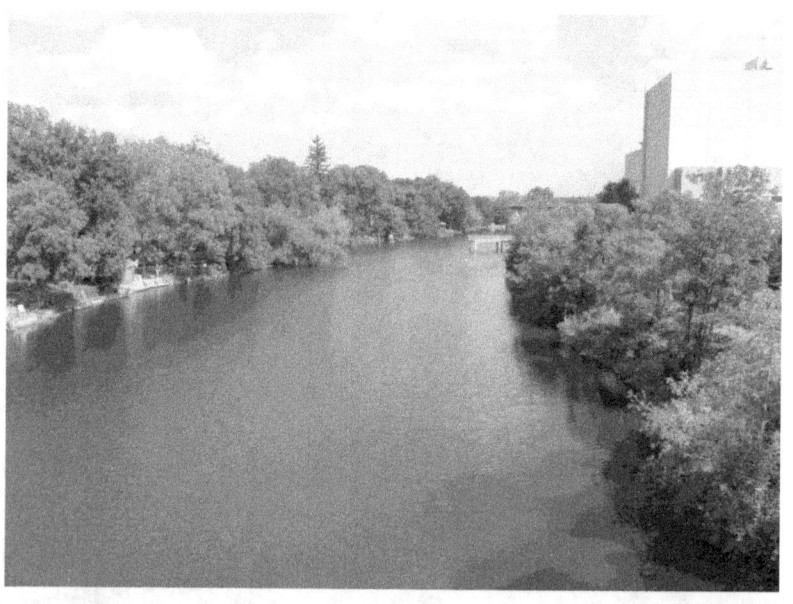

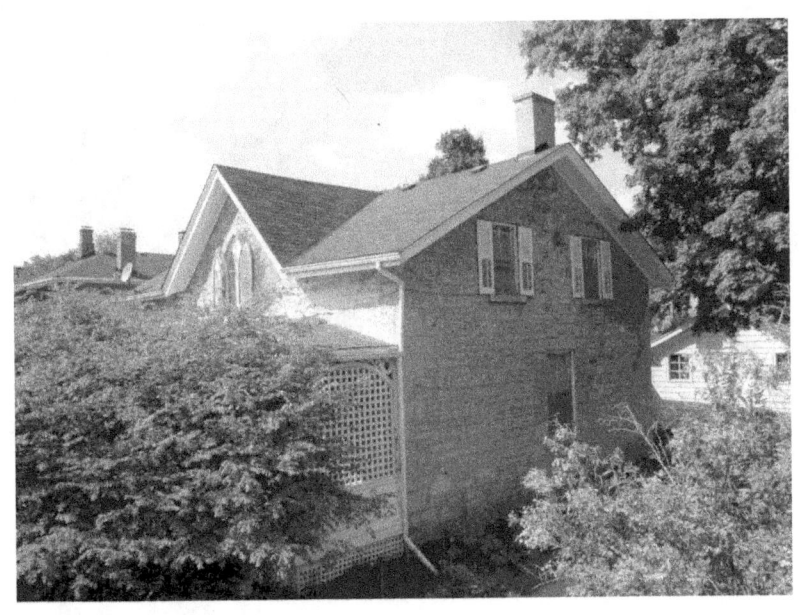

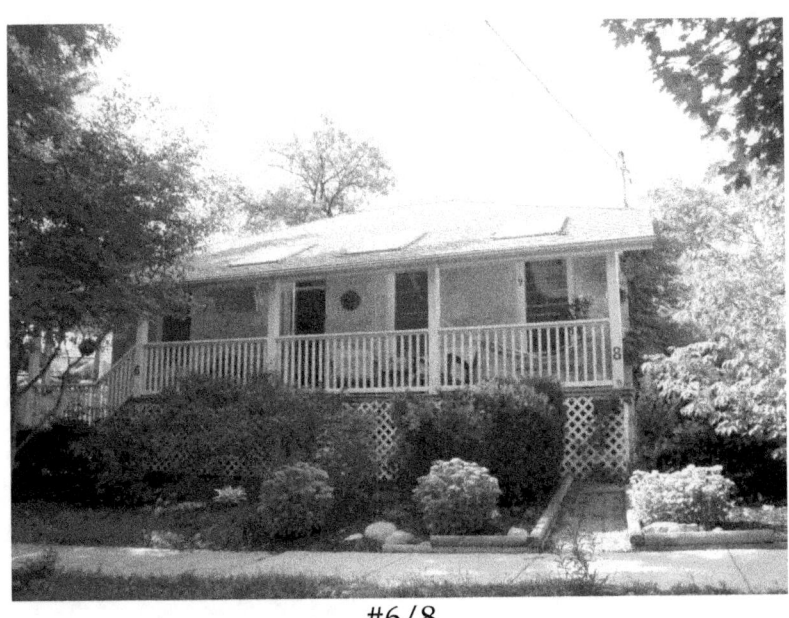

#6/8

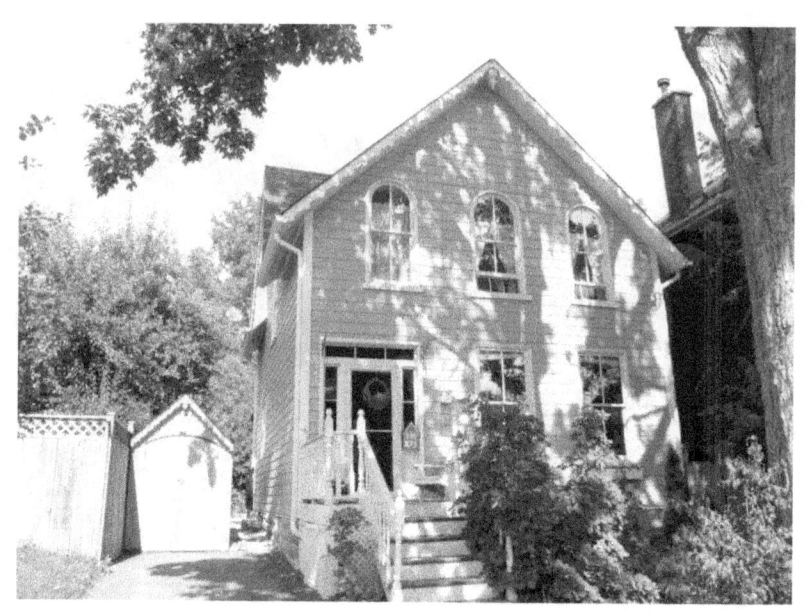

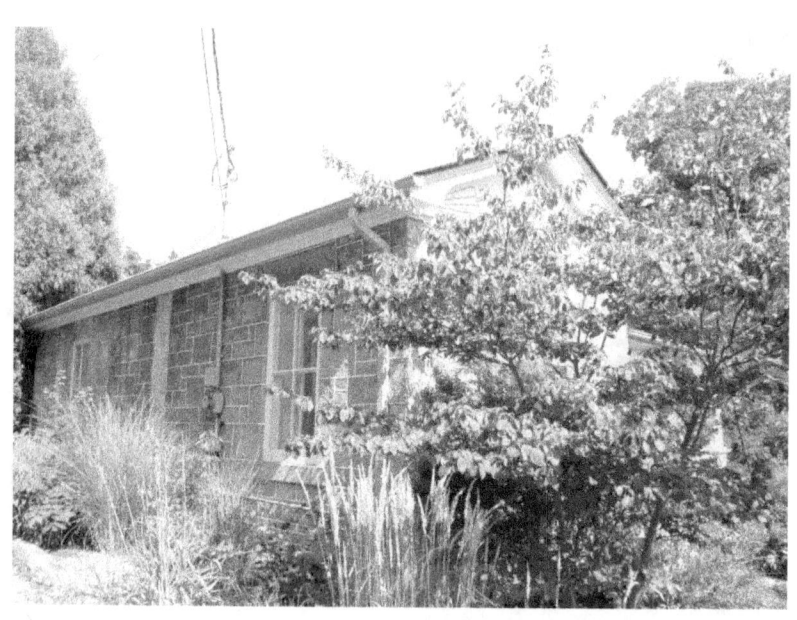

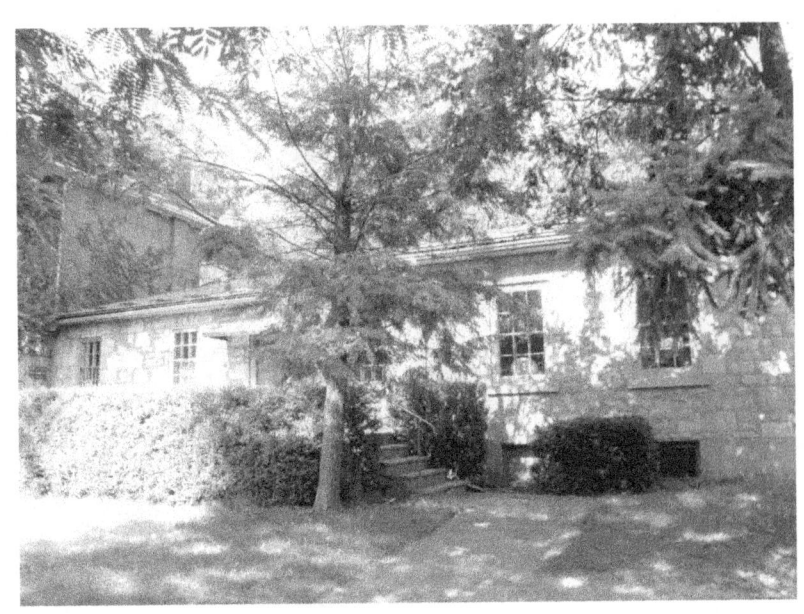

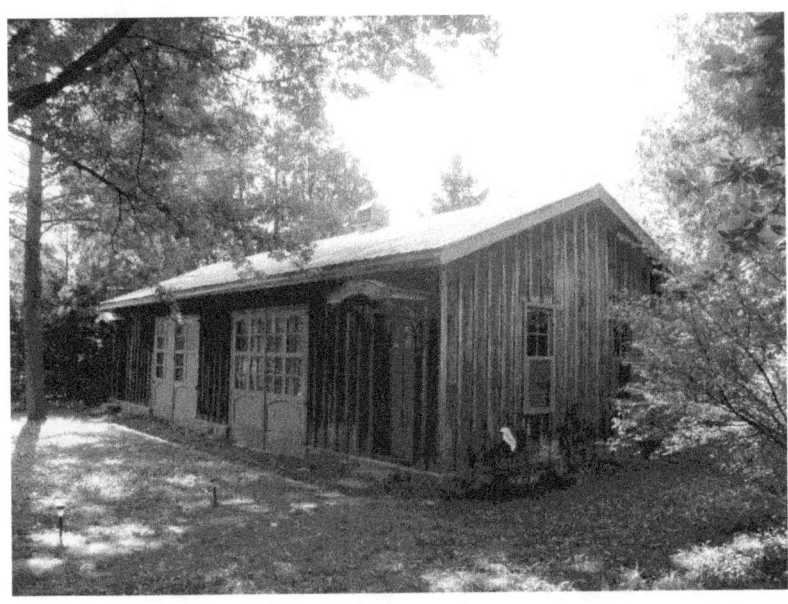

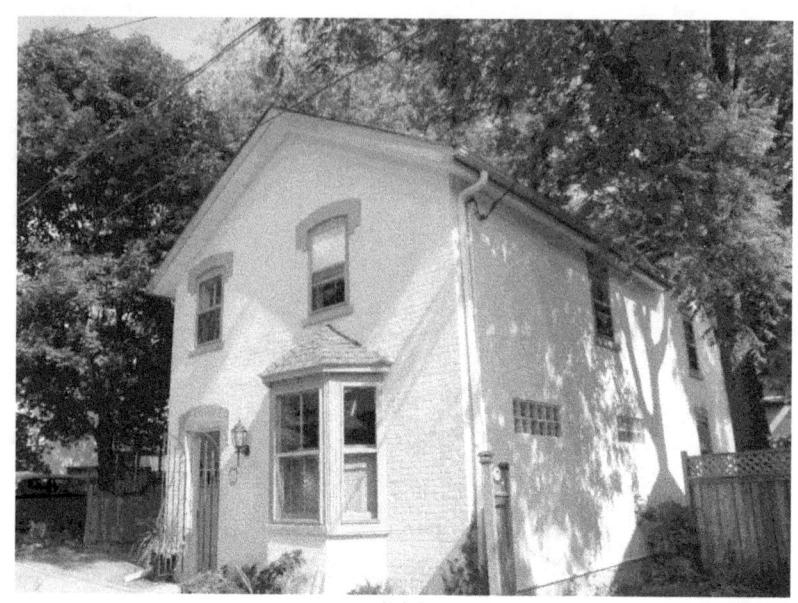

#11

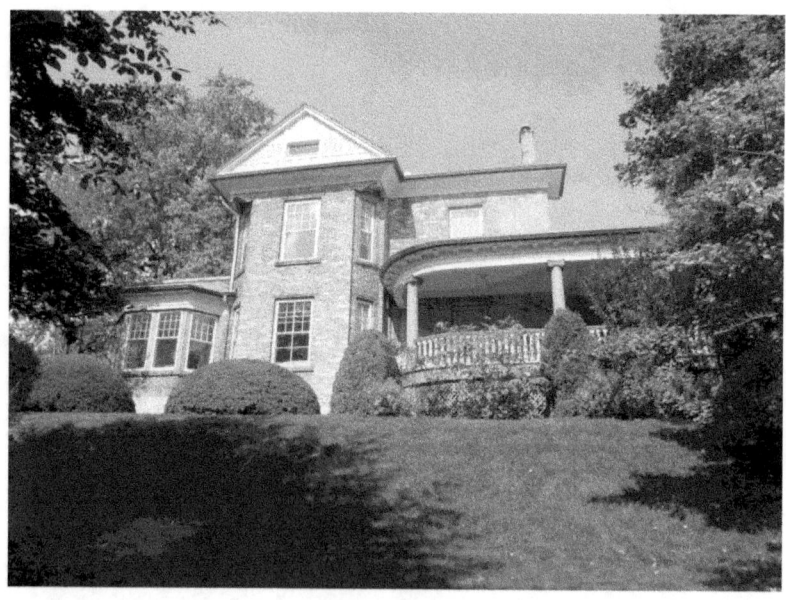

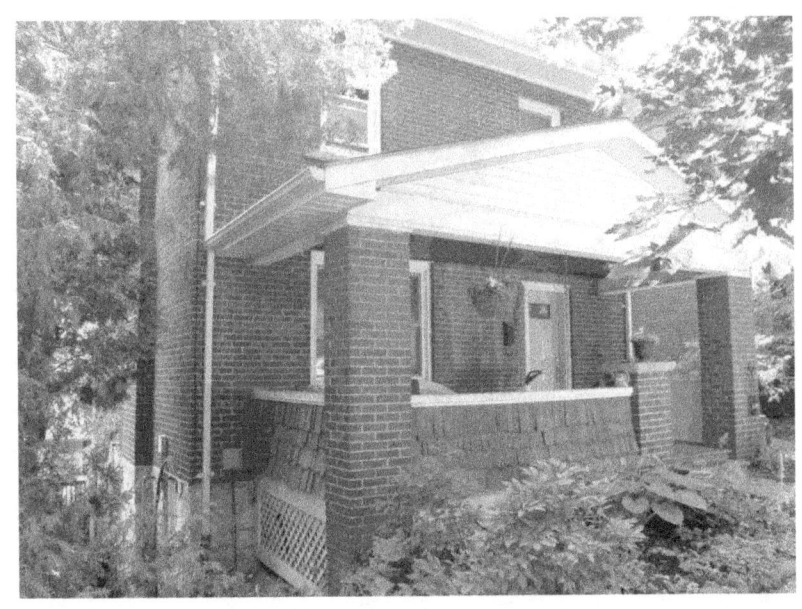

#40 – stone basement

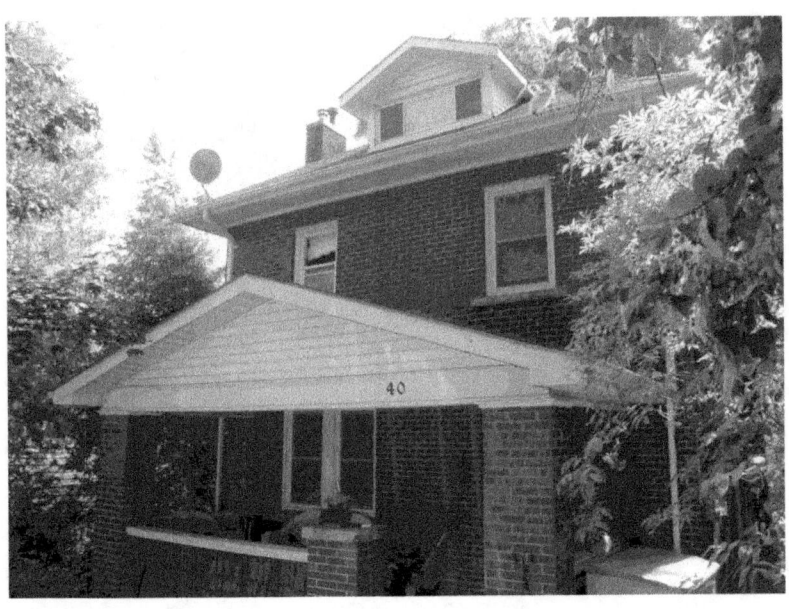

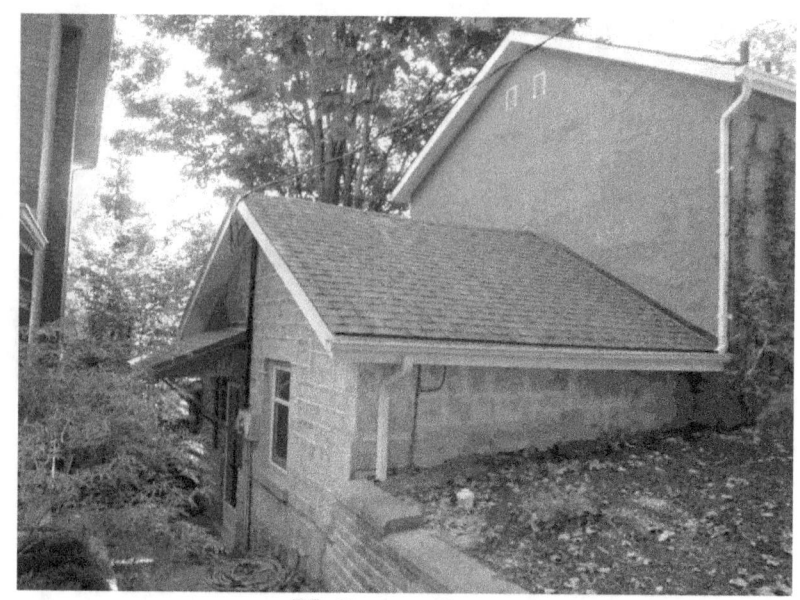

58 Queen Street

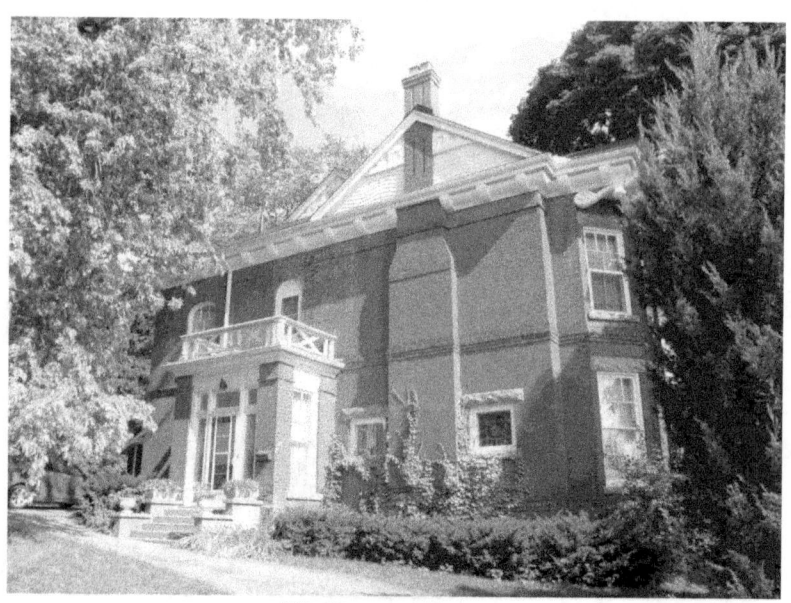

55 Queen Street

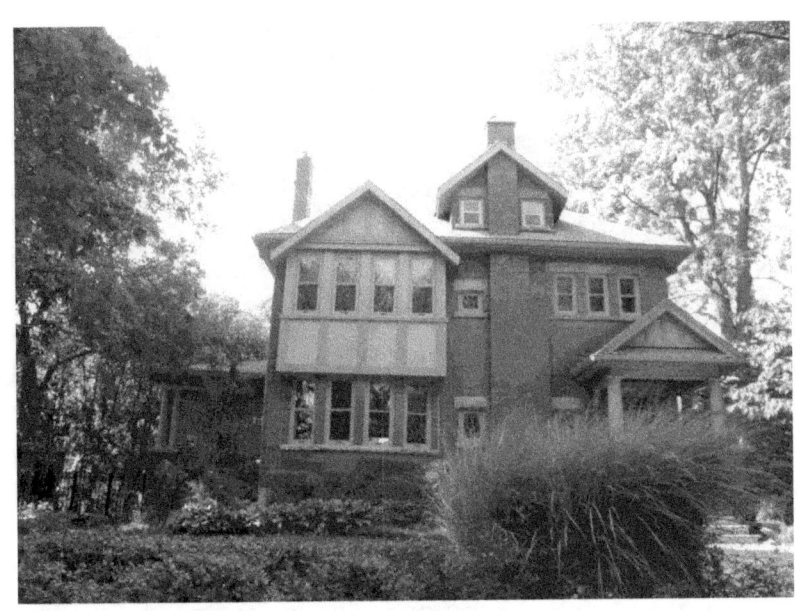

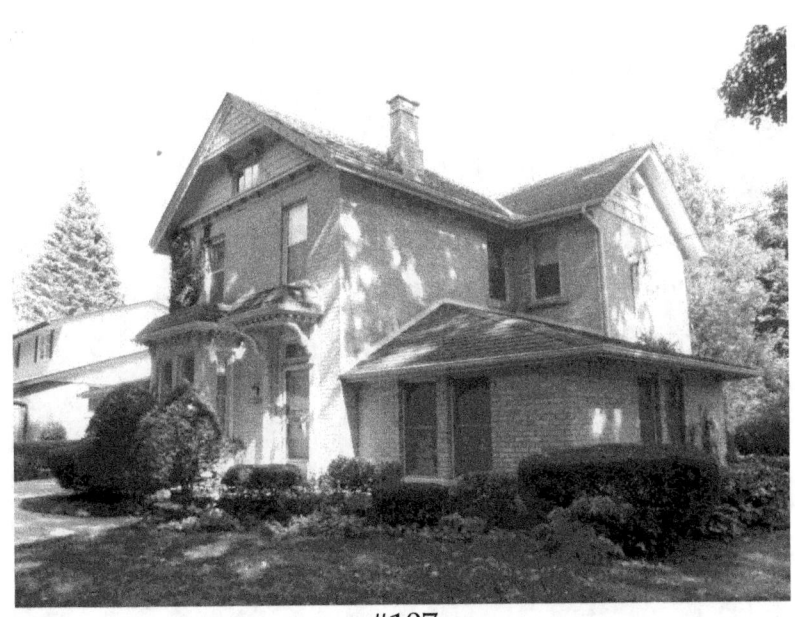

#107

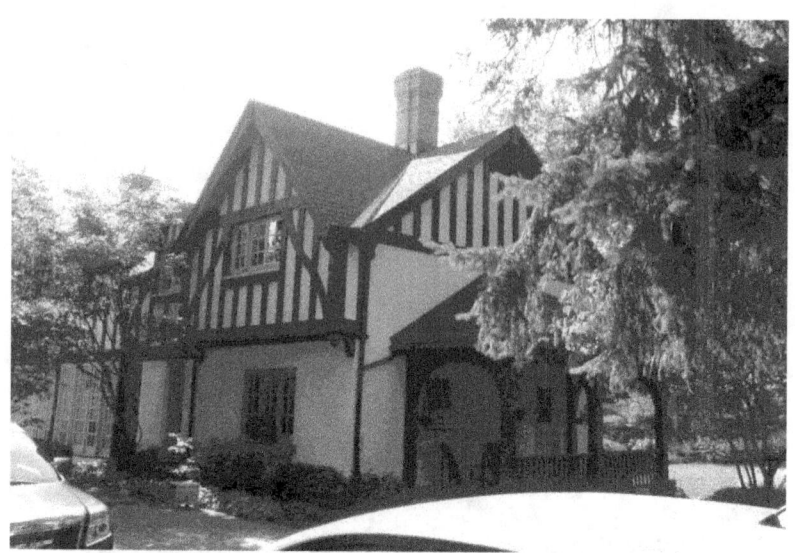

26 Stuart Street – Ker Cavan
Coach House built 1928-29 in the Tudor Revival style
As part of the expansion of Ker Cavan

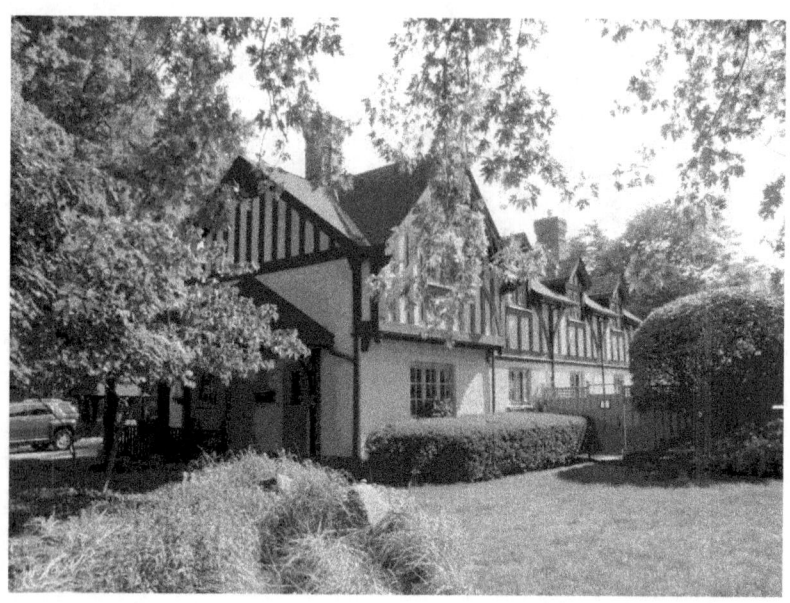

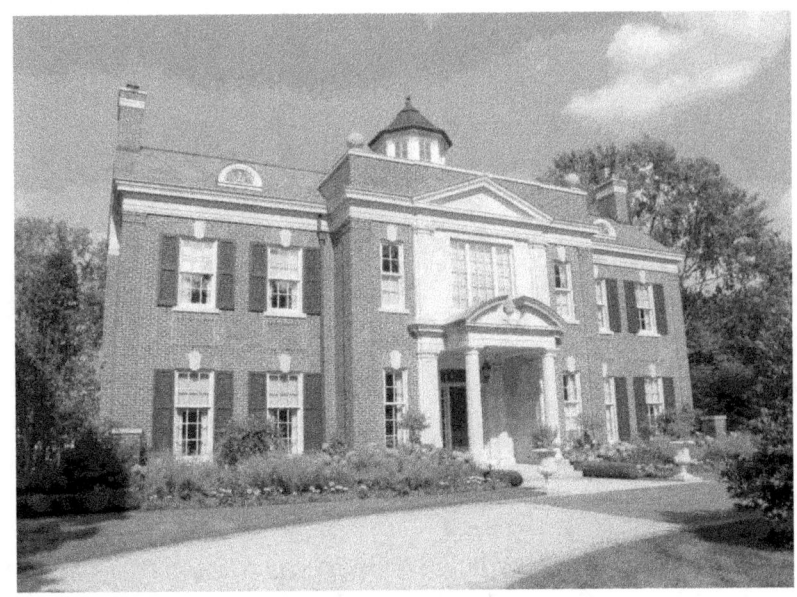
21 Stuart Street
Georgian style

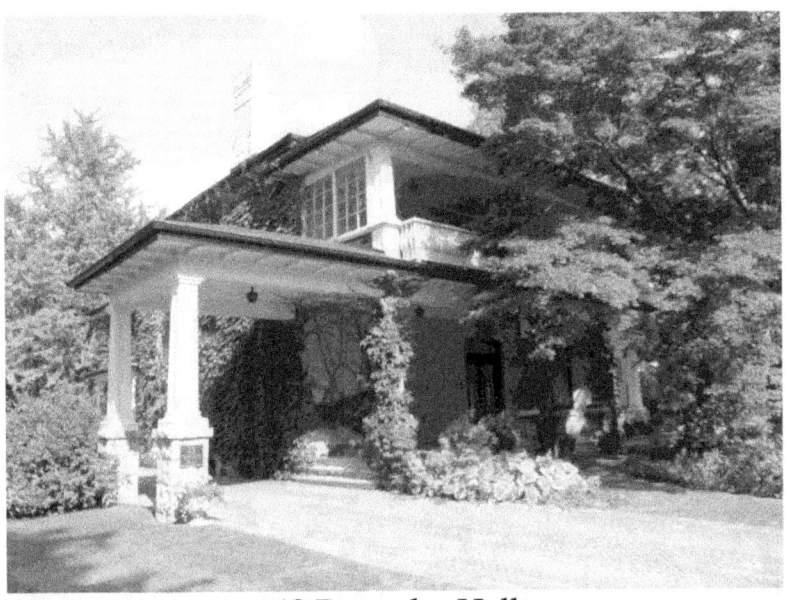
13 Duncolm Hall

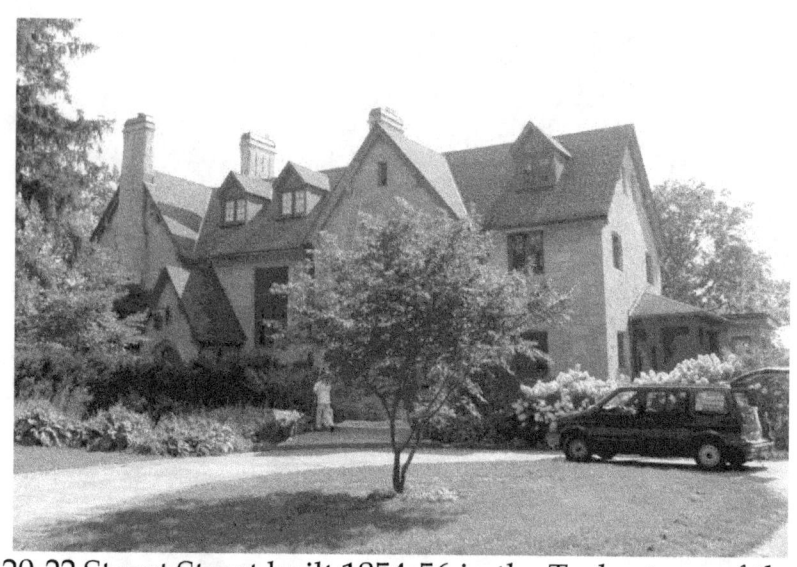

20-22 Stuart Street built 1854-56 in the Tudor type of the Gothic Revival style
Expanded and renamed Ker Cavan in 1925-28

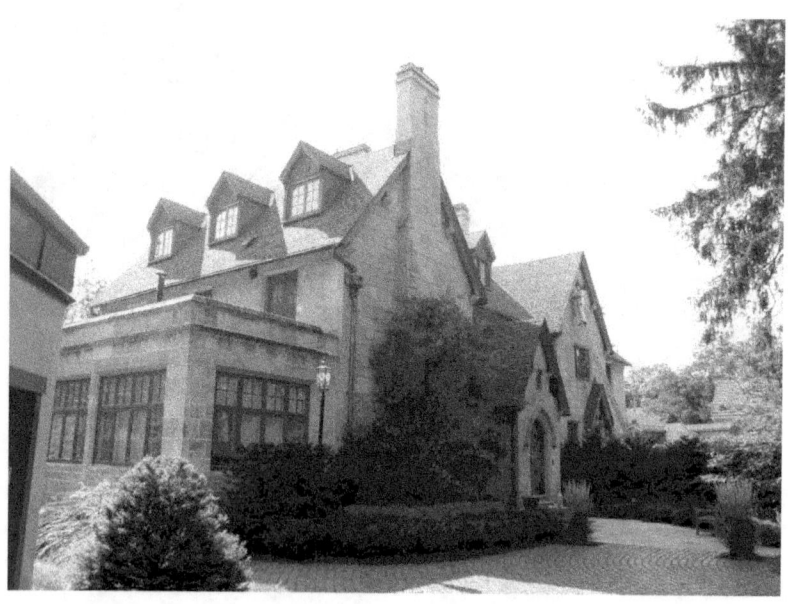

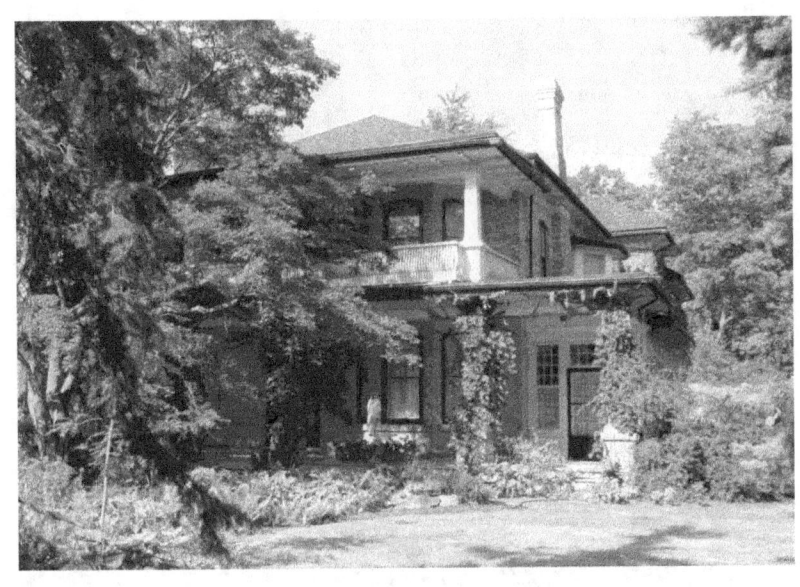

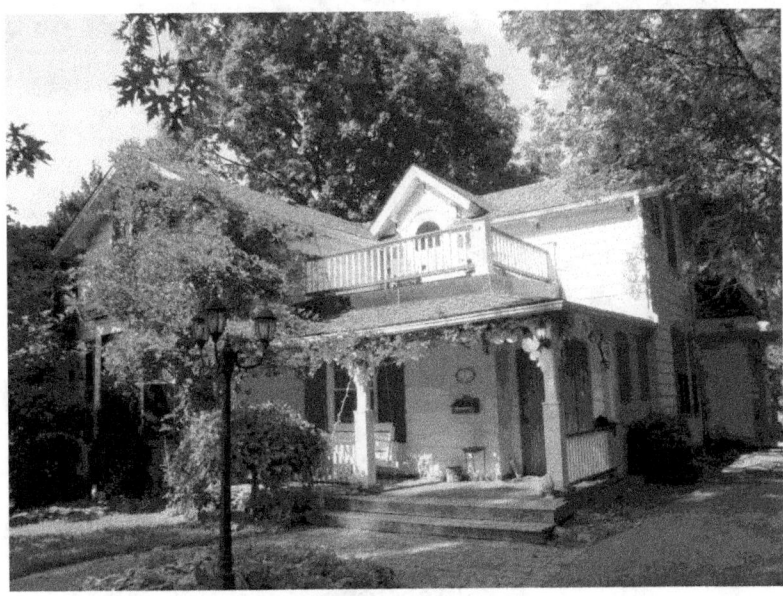

7 Stuart Street

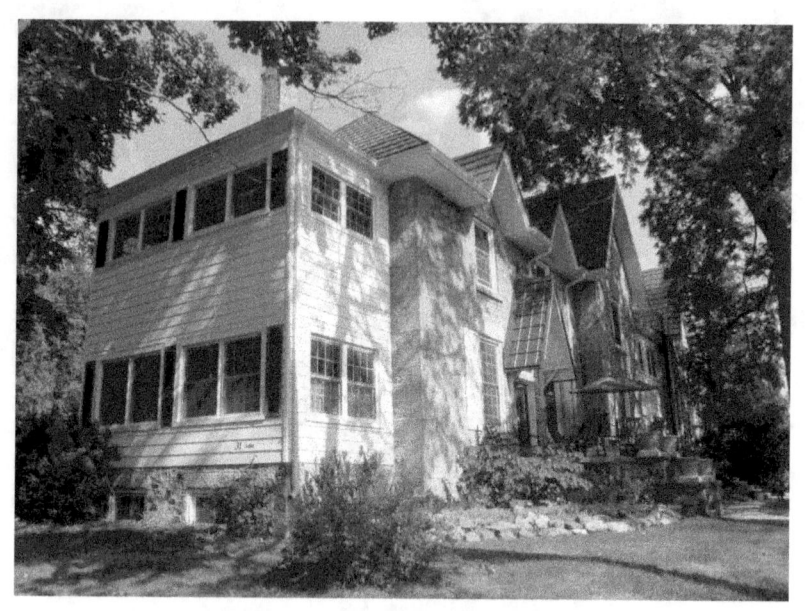

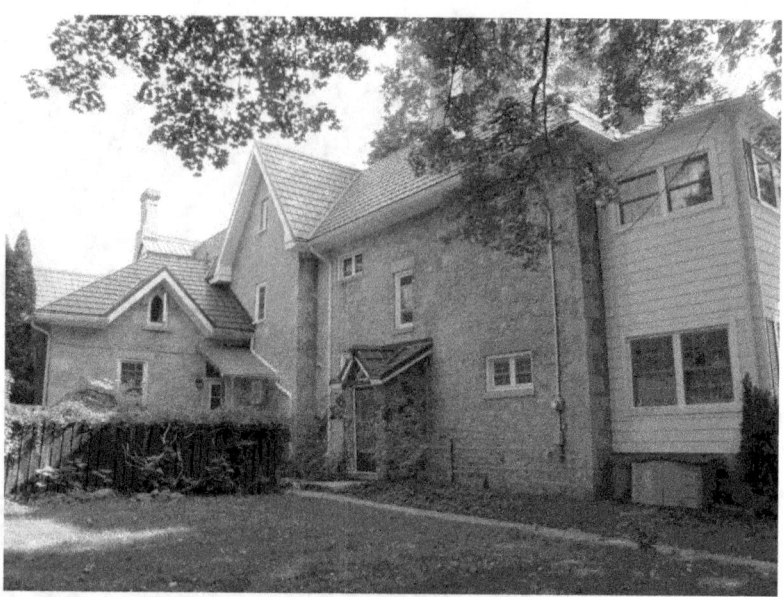

limestone

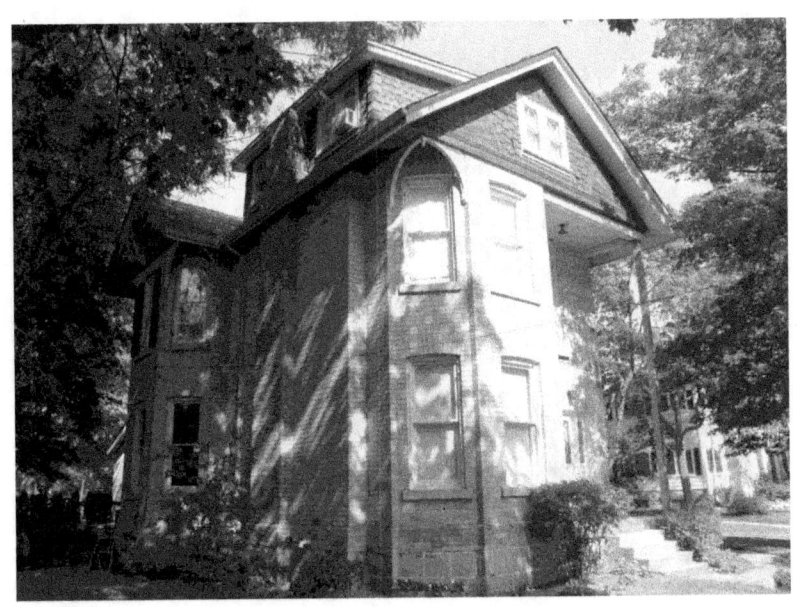

Local yellow brick

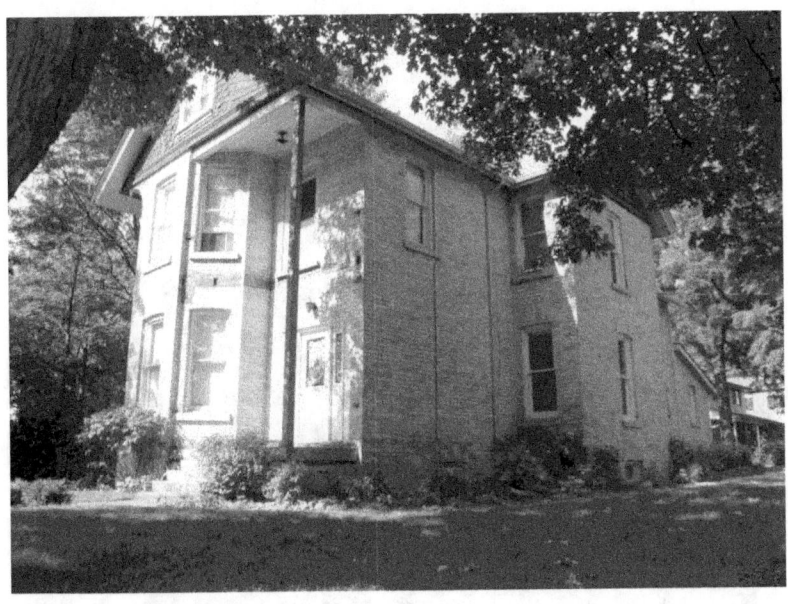

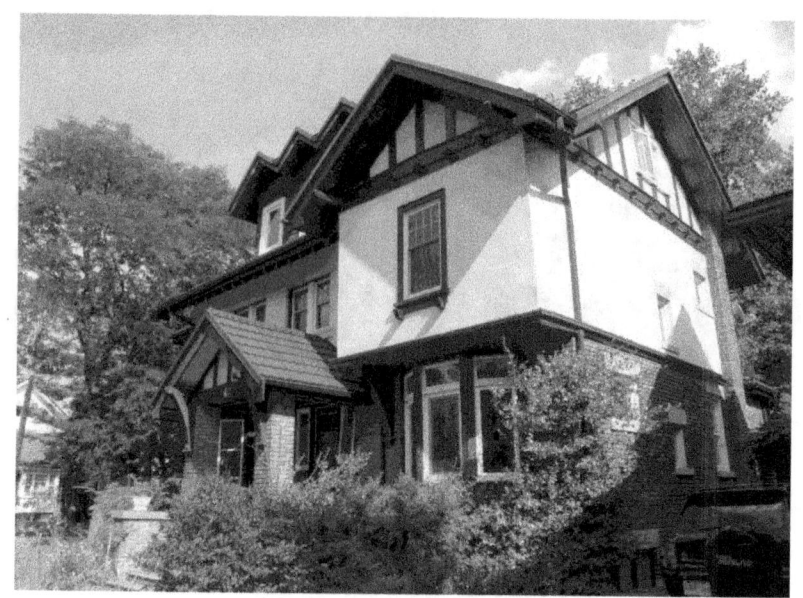

Tudor style

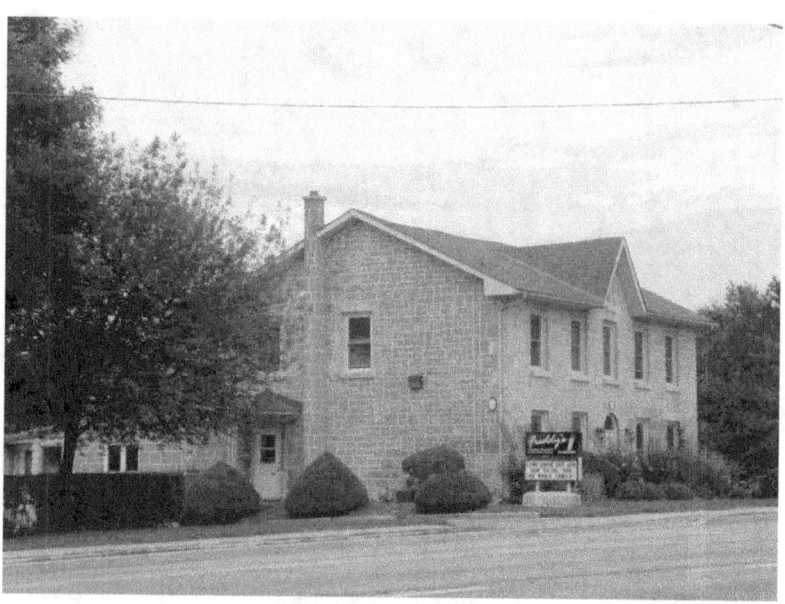

#414 – limestone

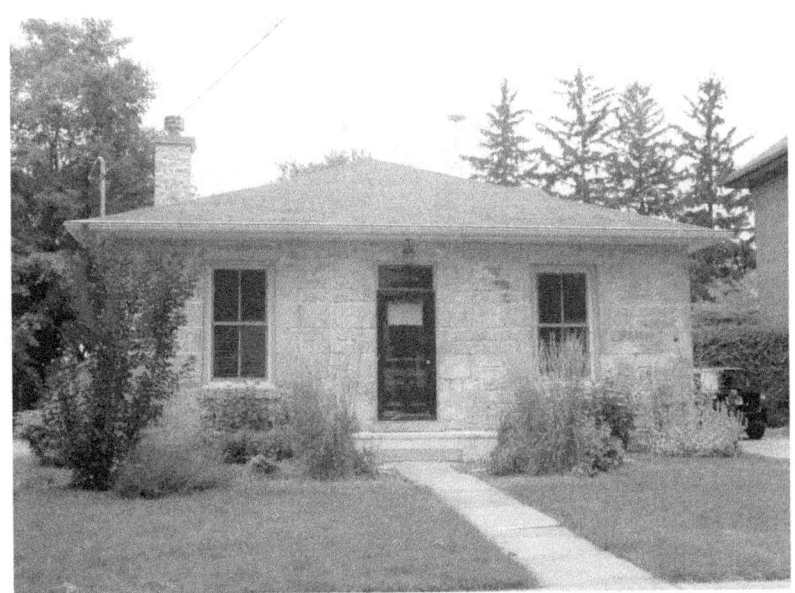

#29 – limestone cottage

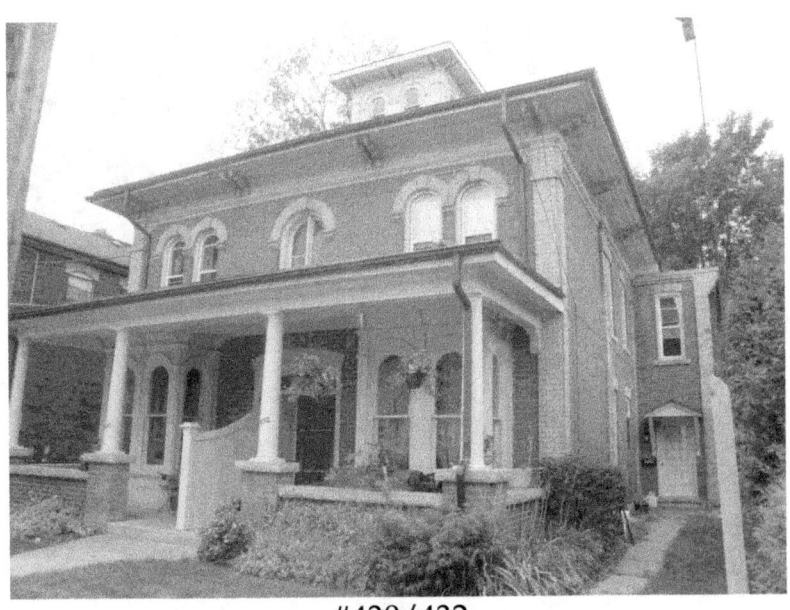

#430/432

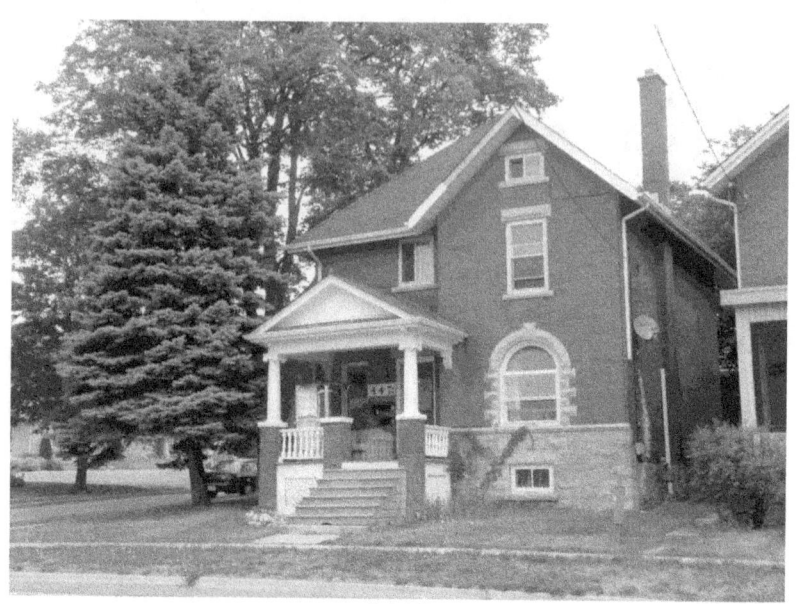

#447

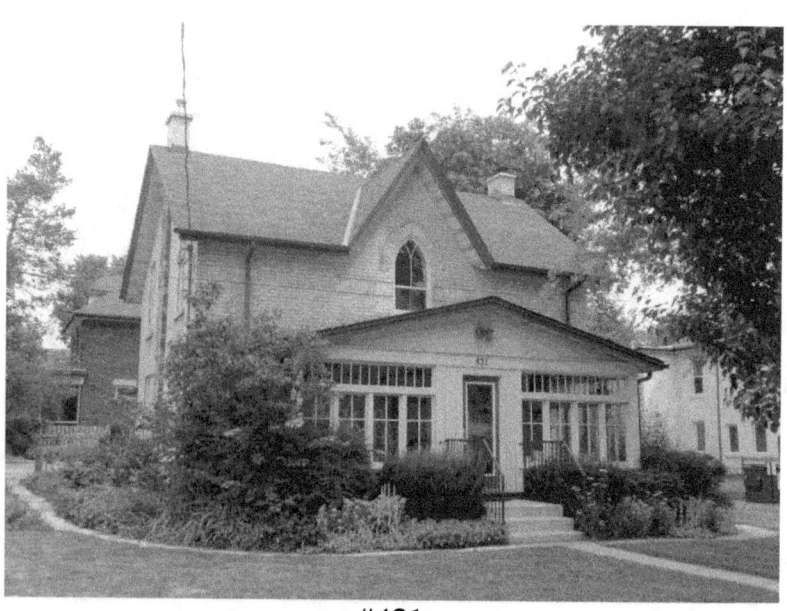

#421

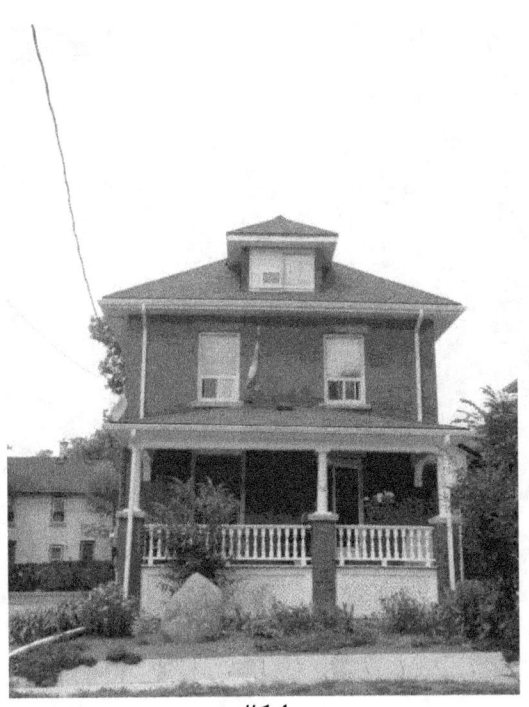

#14

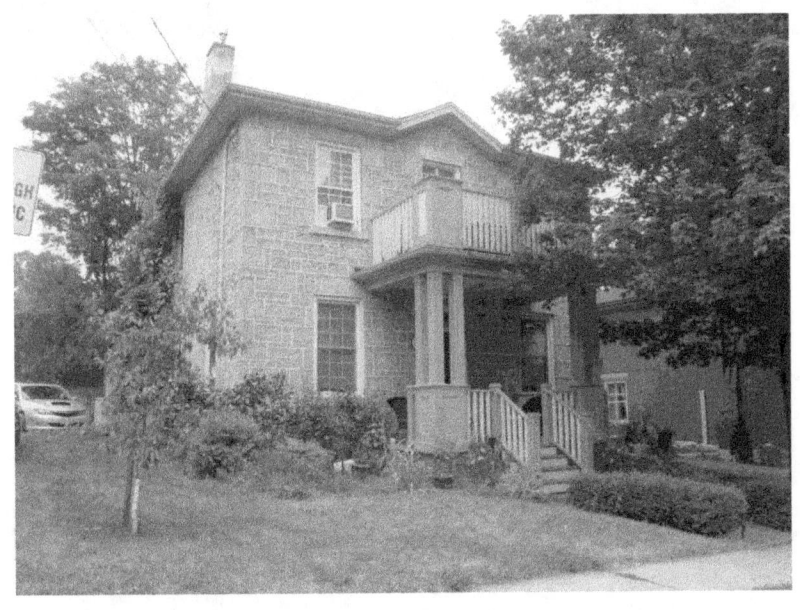

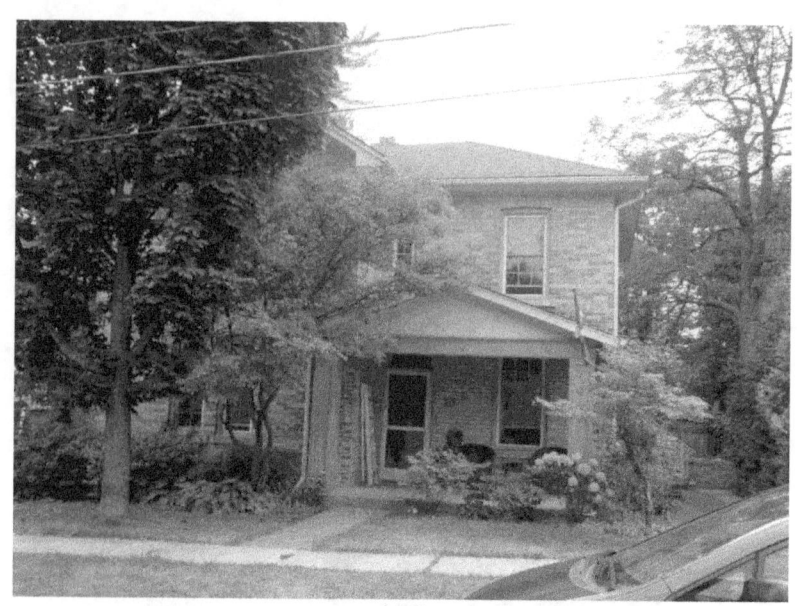

#19

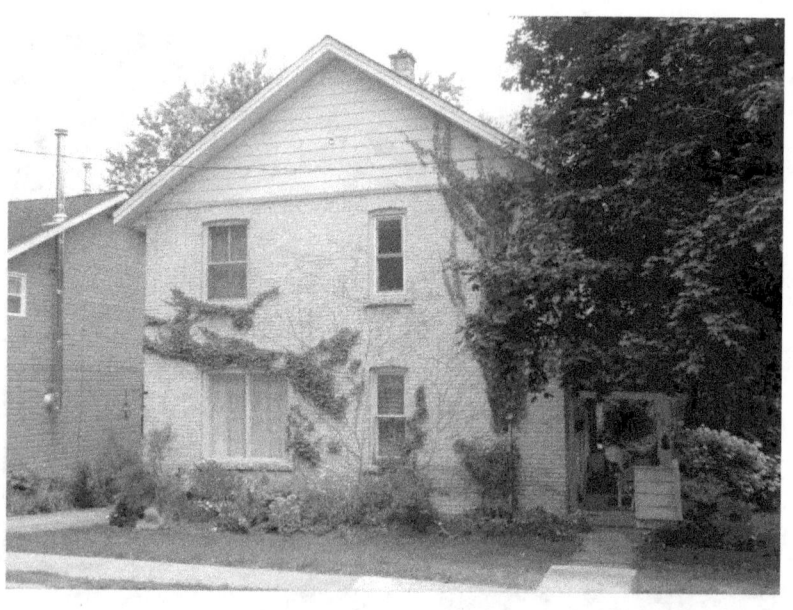

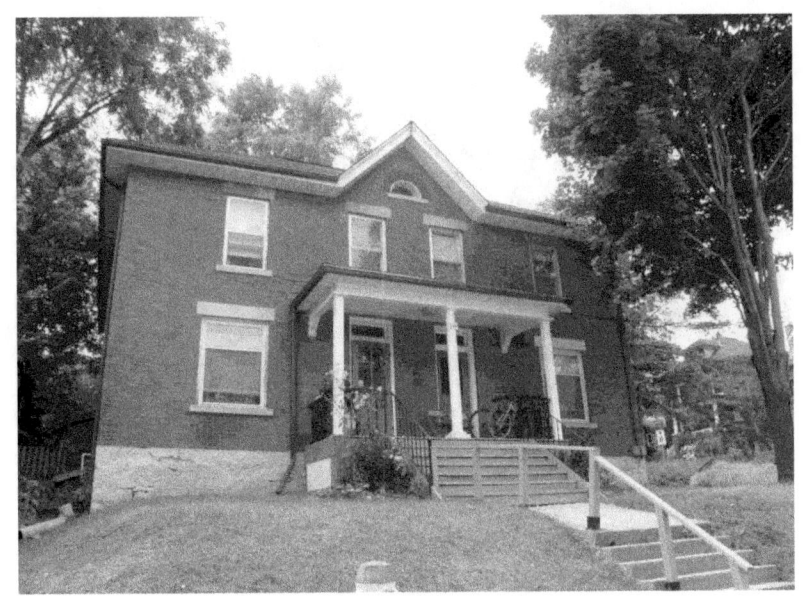

#116

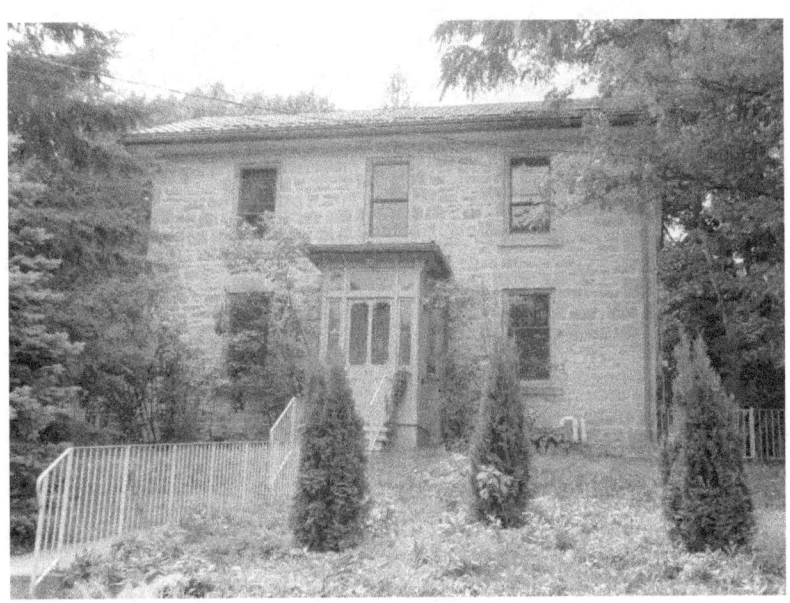

#112

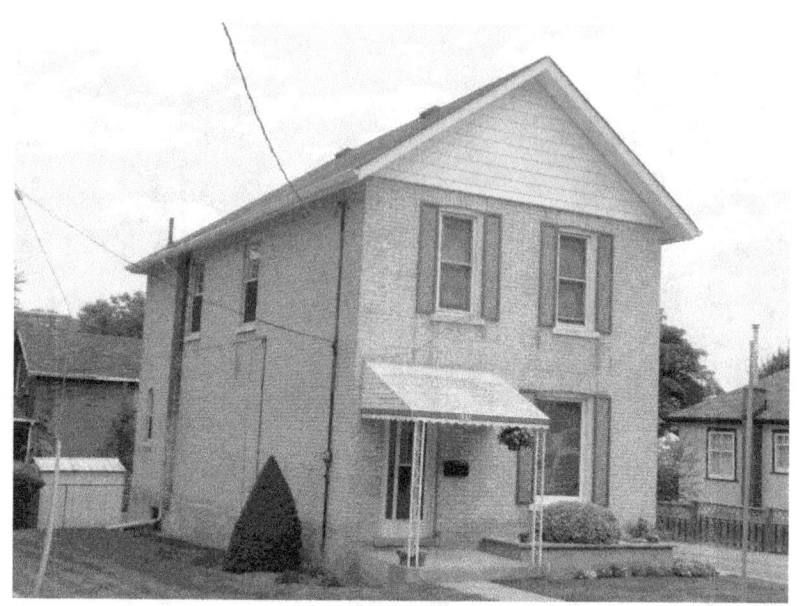

#101

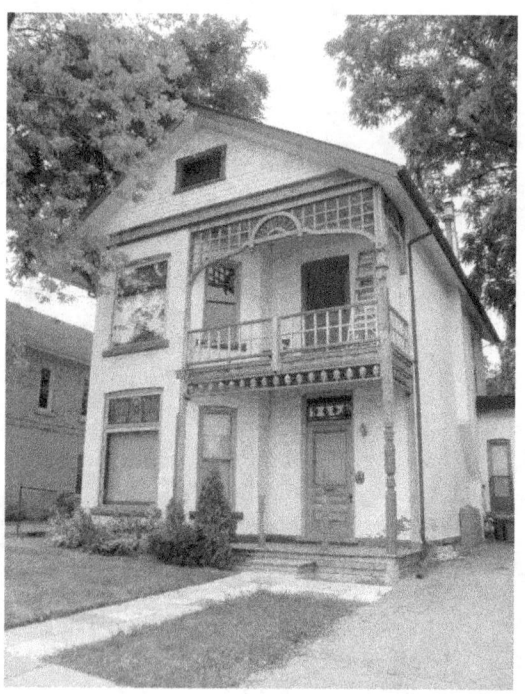

#6

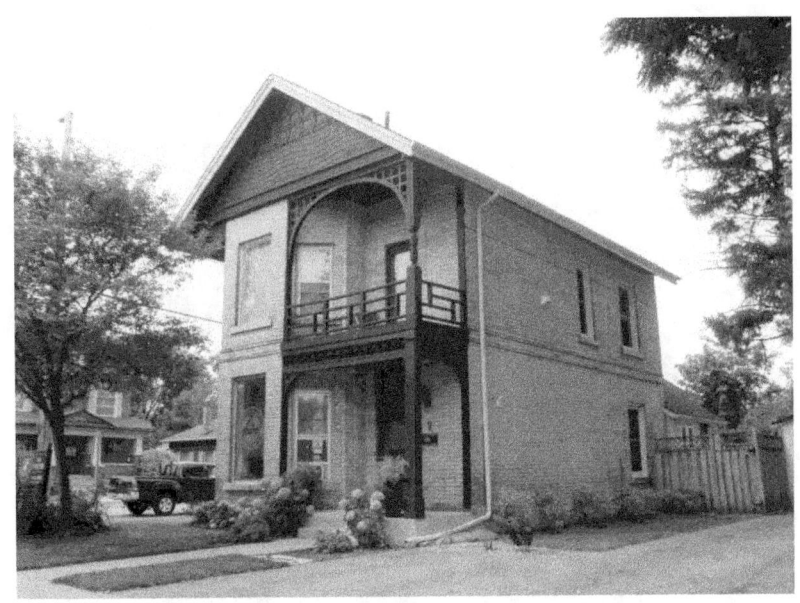

#2

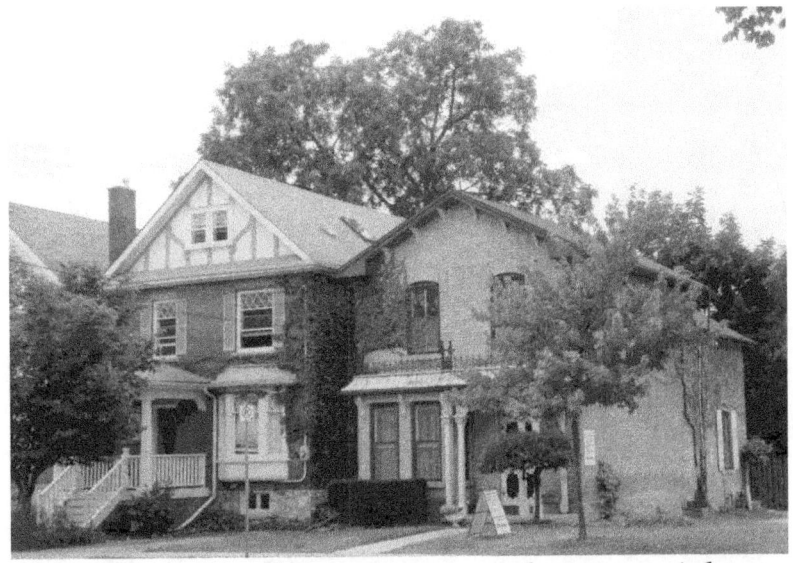

Iron cresting above entrance on house on right

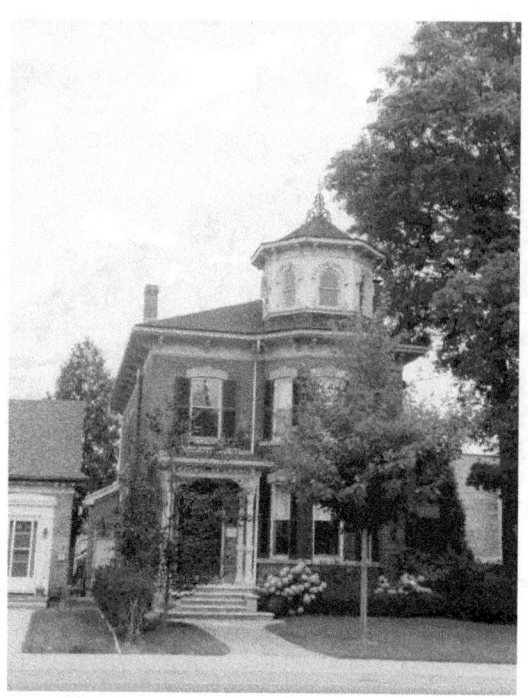

Bay windows on both storeys, plus hexagonal dormer on top

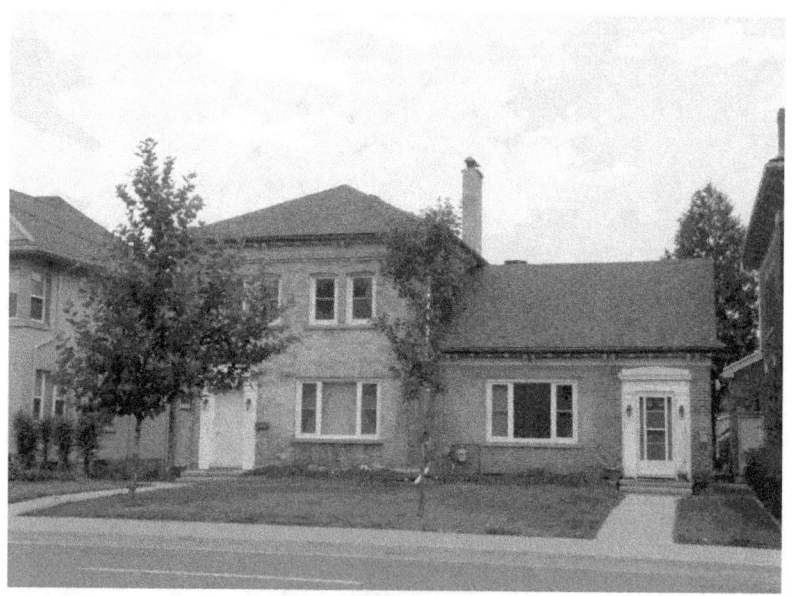

265 Woolwich Street

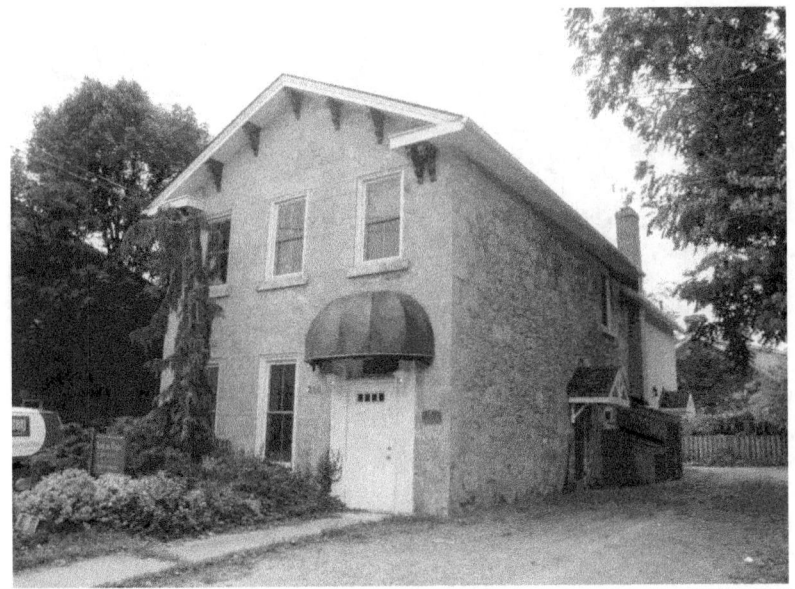

258 Woolwich Street – main stone portion built 1871-72
Single brackets on cornice return

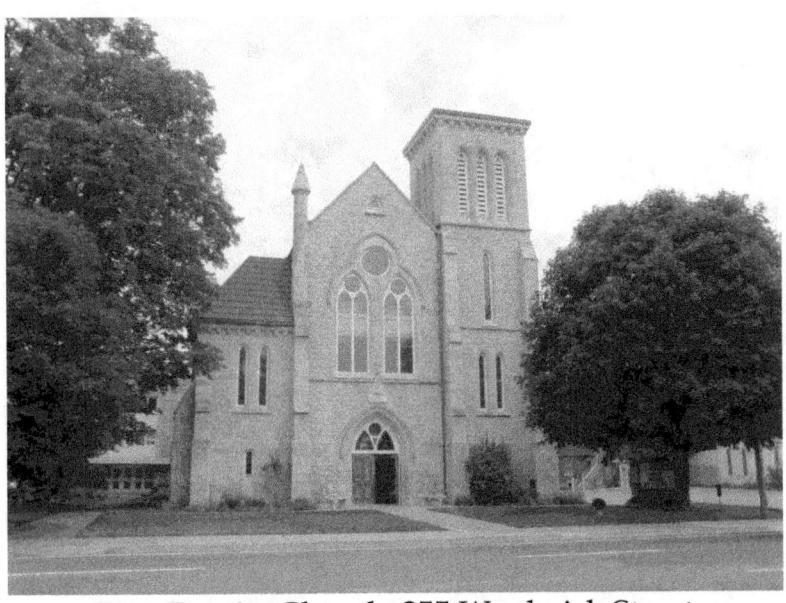

First Baptist Church, 255 Woolwich Street

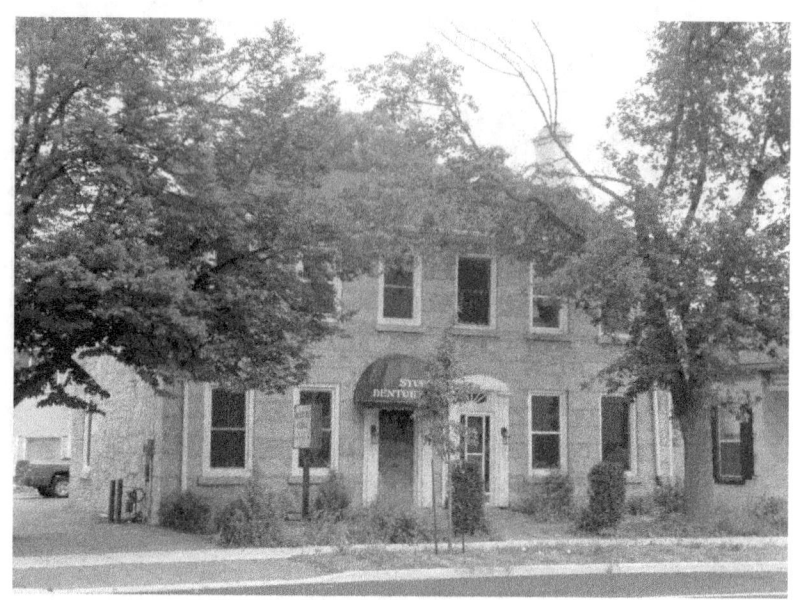

191 Woolwich Street

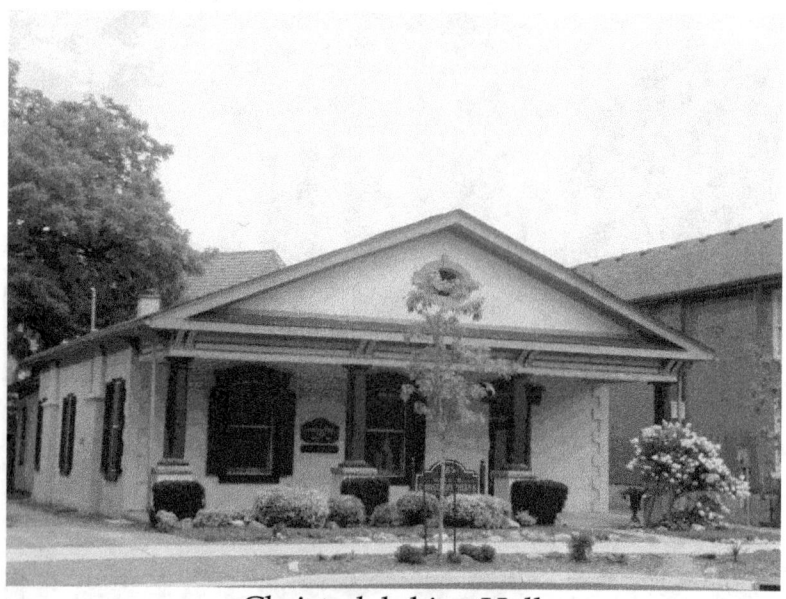

Christadelphian Hall
187 Woolwich Street

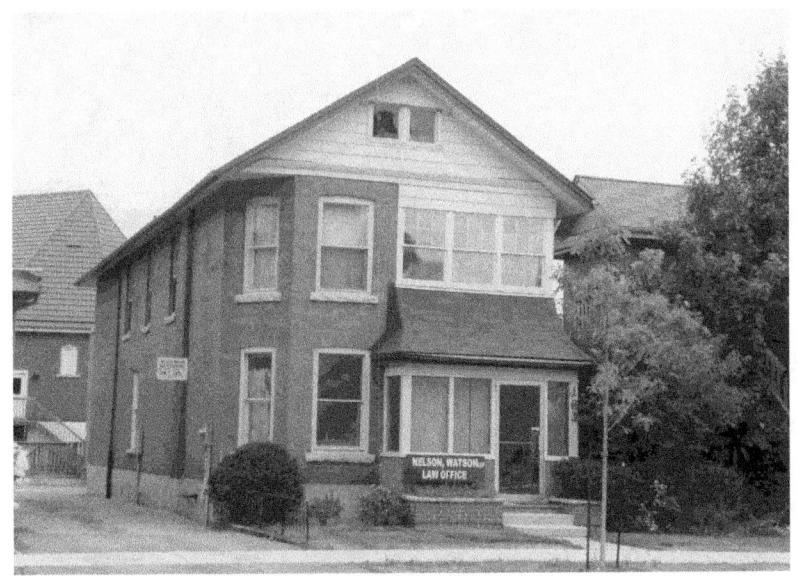

183 Woolwich Street

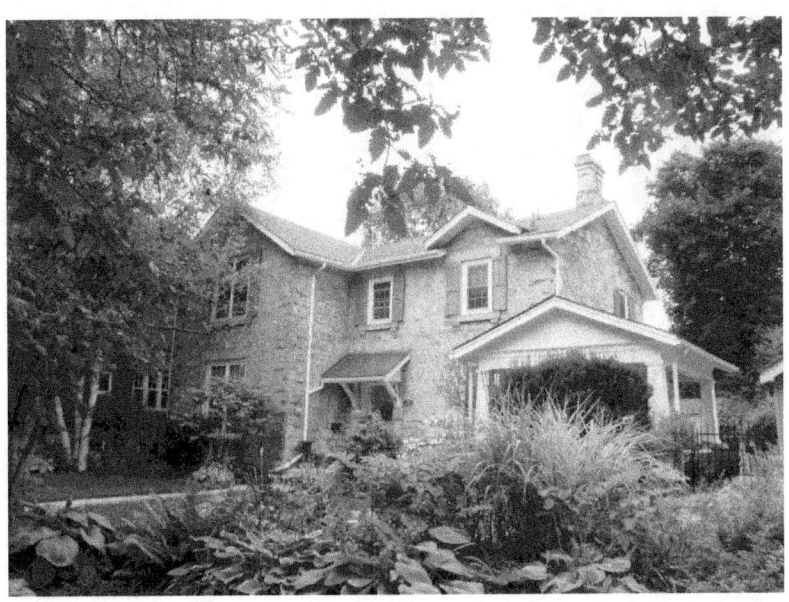

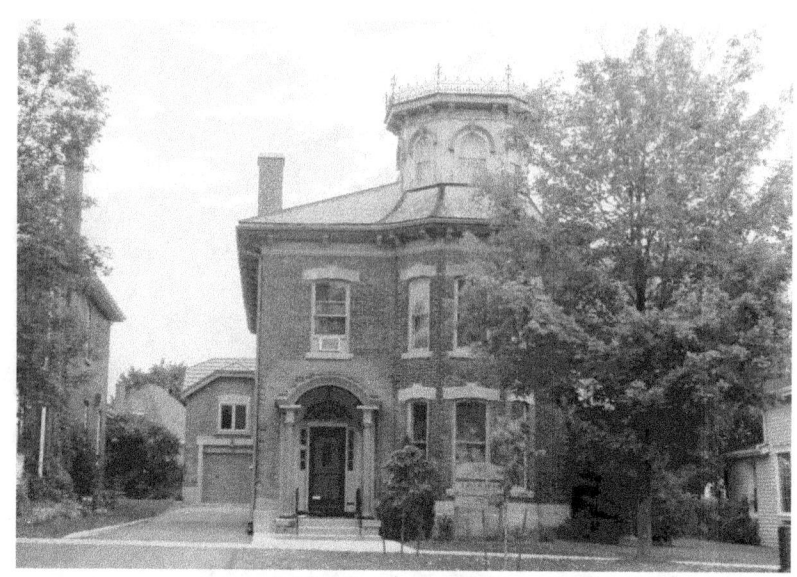

143 Norfolk Street
Iron cresting above hexagonal gable

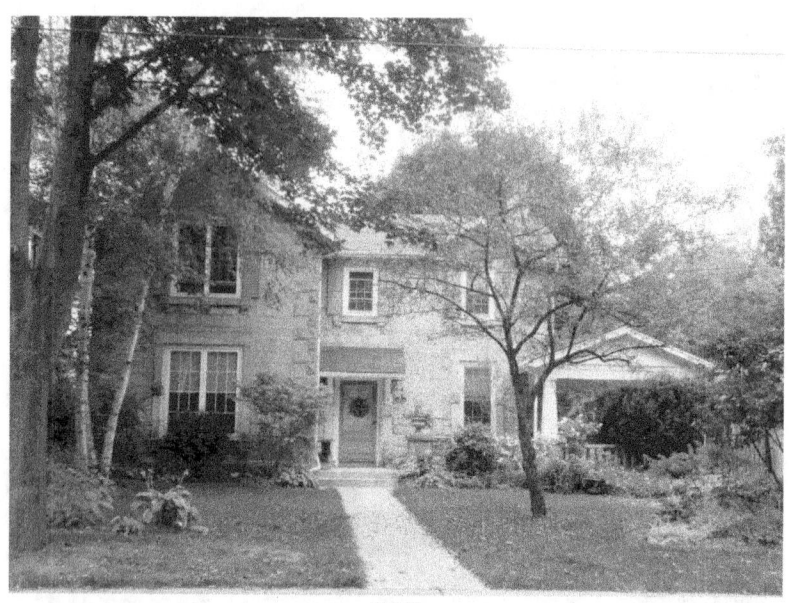

#15

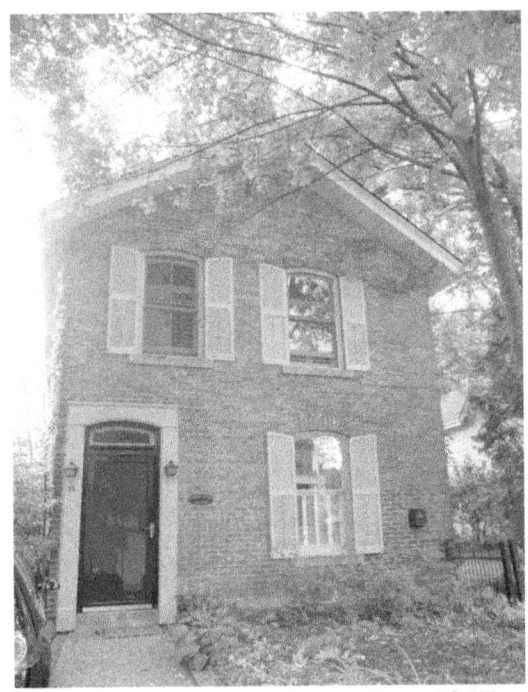

#18 - Donegal House circa 1867

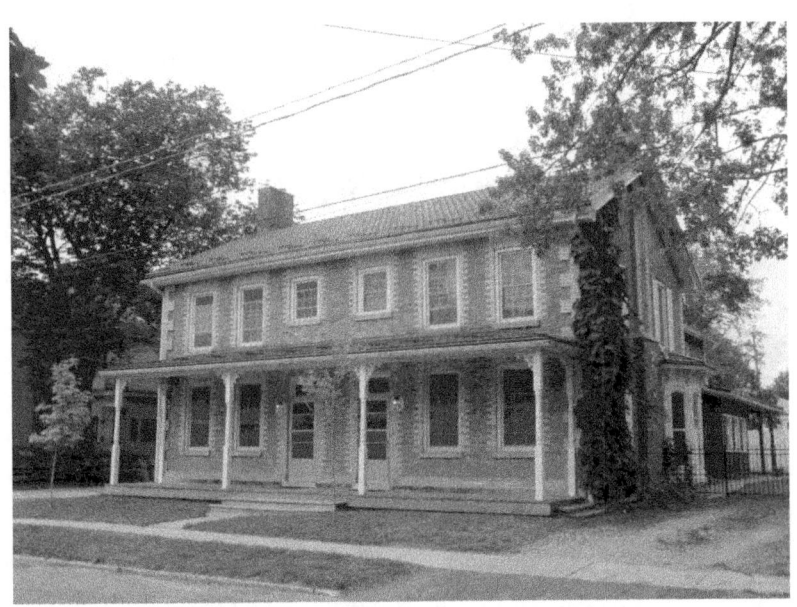

#23/25

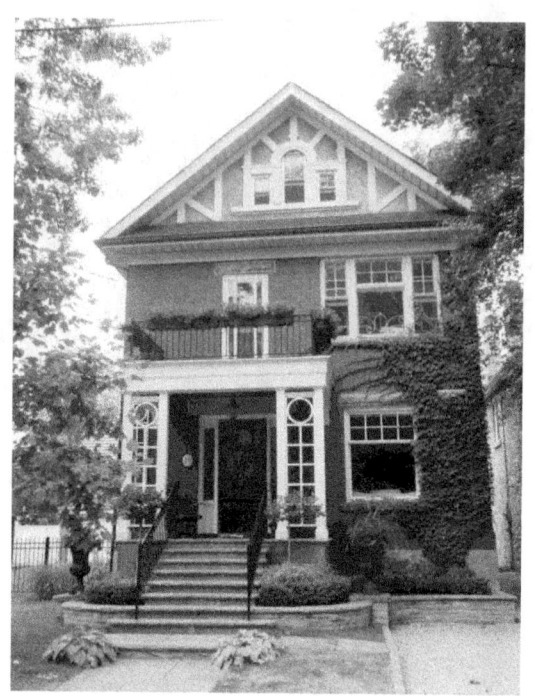

#19 – Tudor style

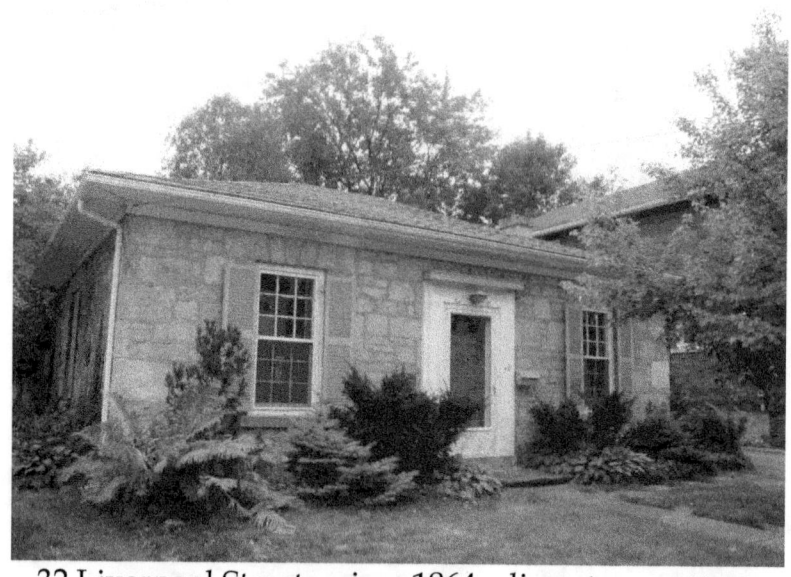

32 Liverpool Street – circa 1864 – limestone cottage

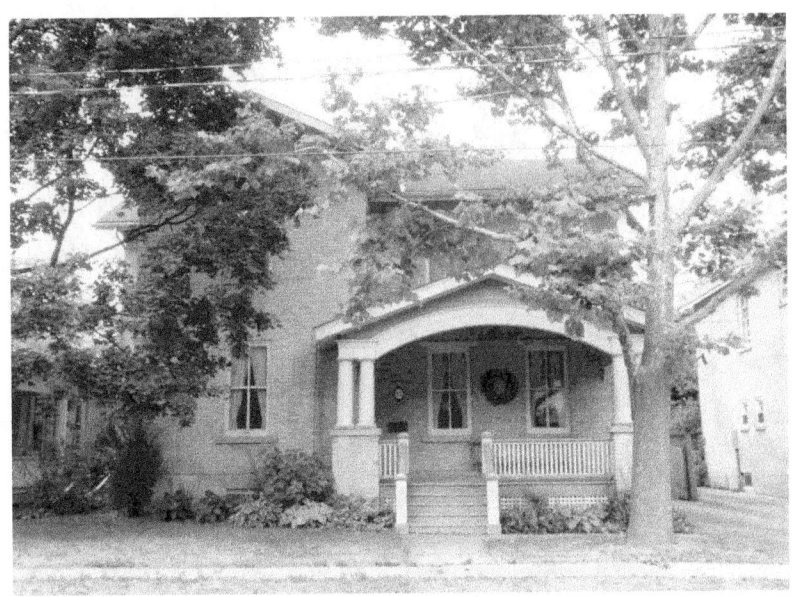

#37

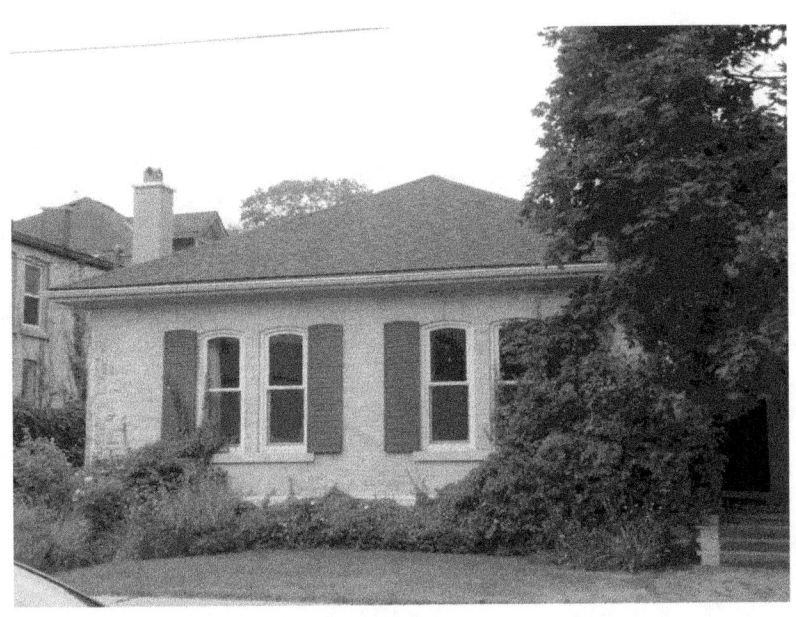

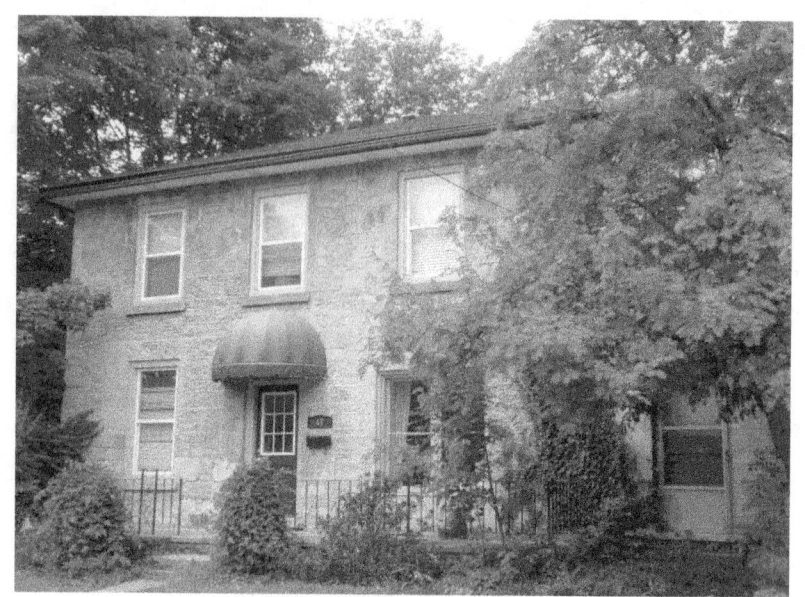

#47

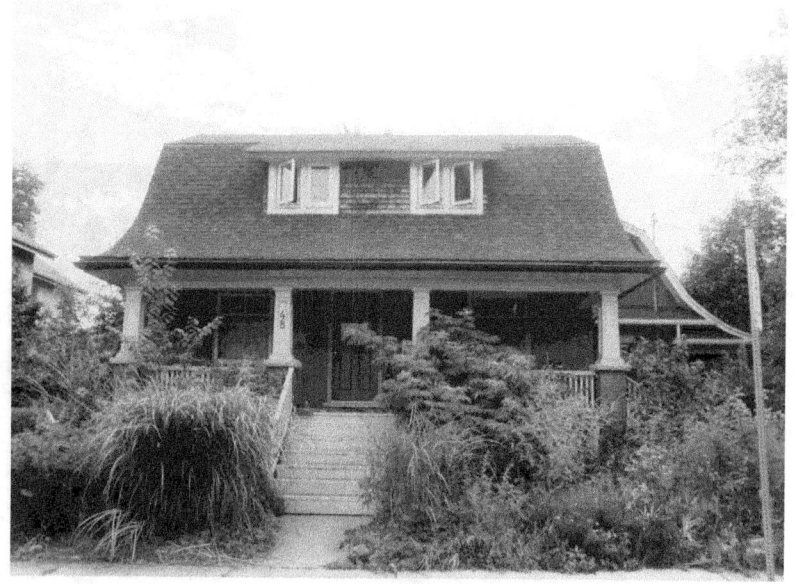

#48

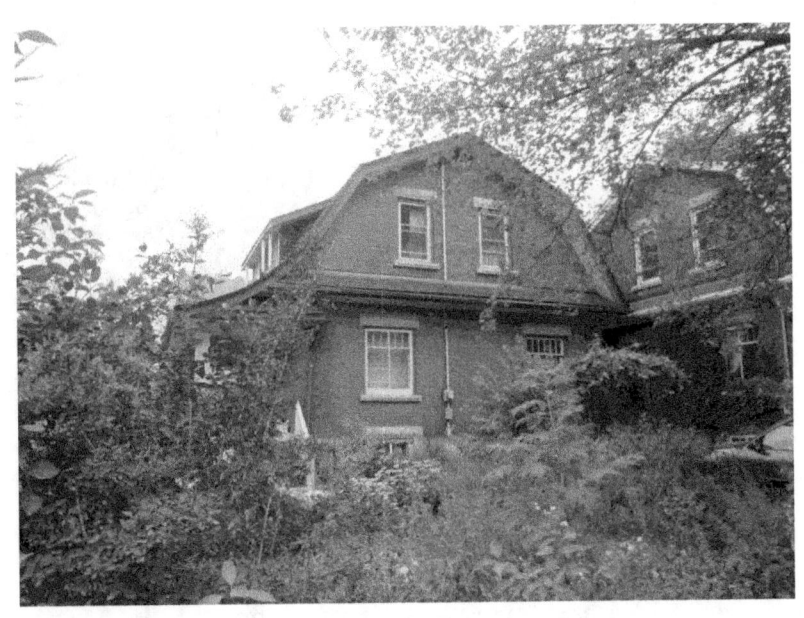

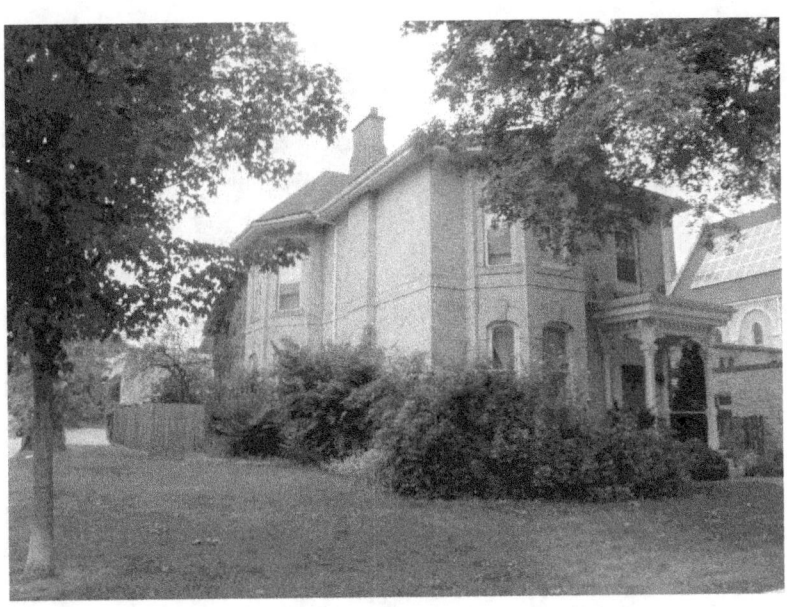

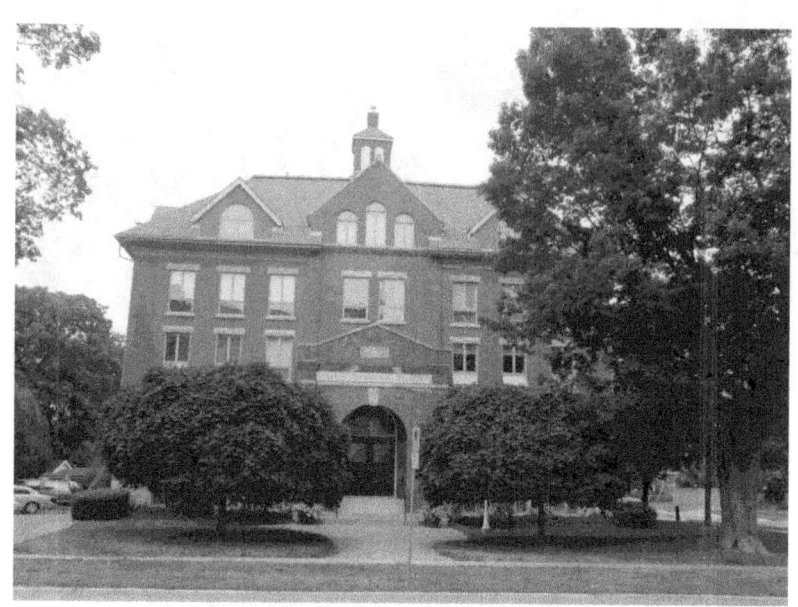

King Edward Place – 1903

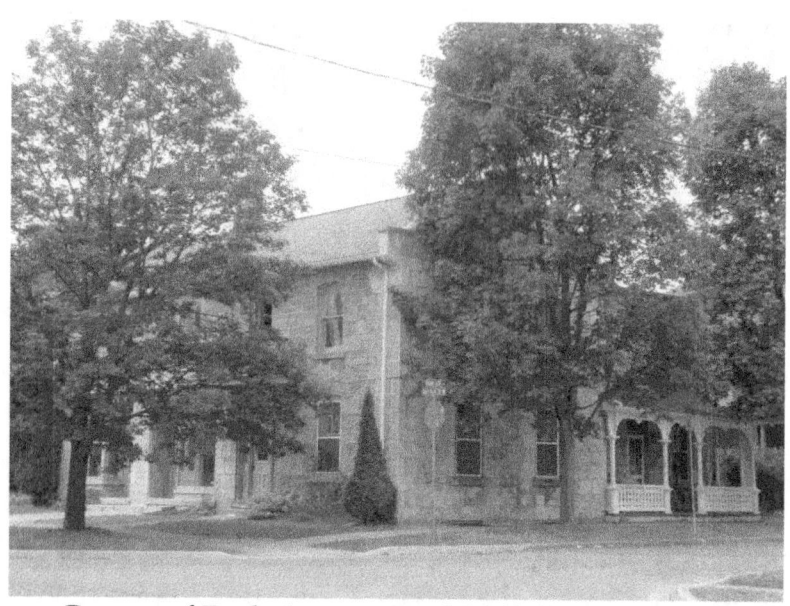

Corner of Park Avenue and Suffolk Street West

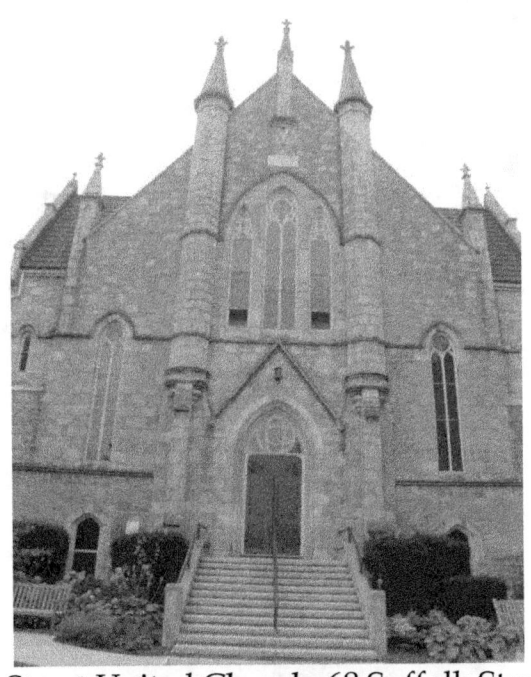

Dublin Street United Church, 68 Suffolk Street West

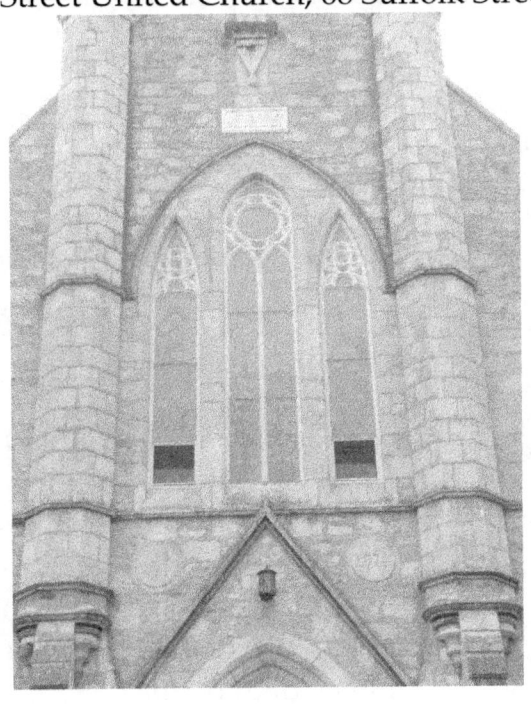

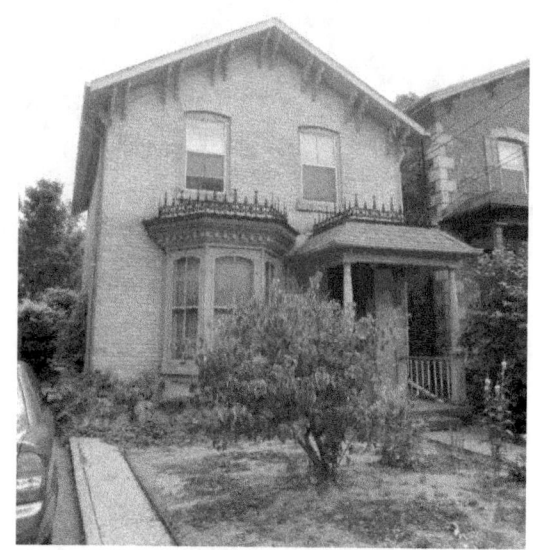

#80 - Paired cornice brackets, iron cresting above bay window and above entranceway

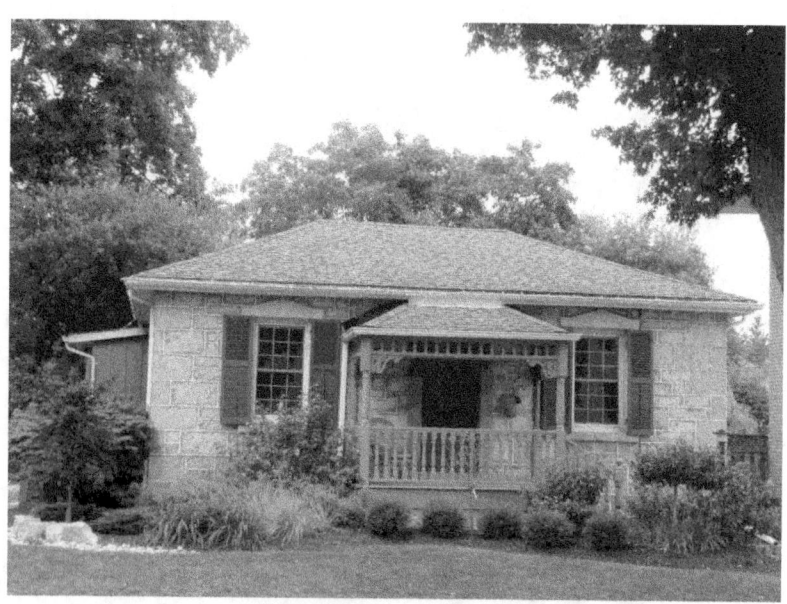

Limestone cottage

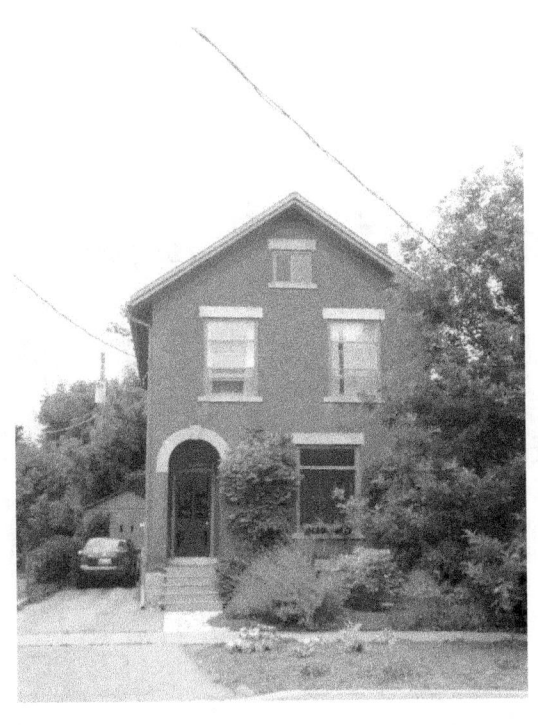

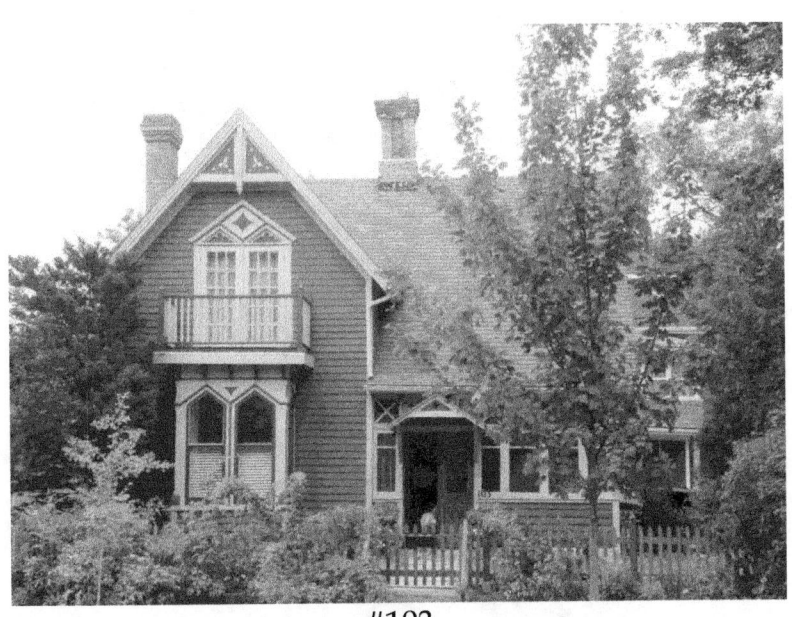

#103

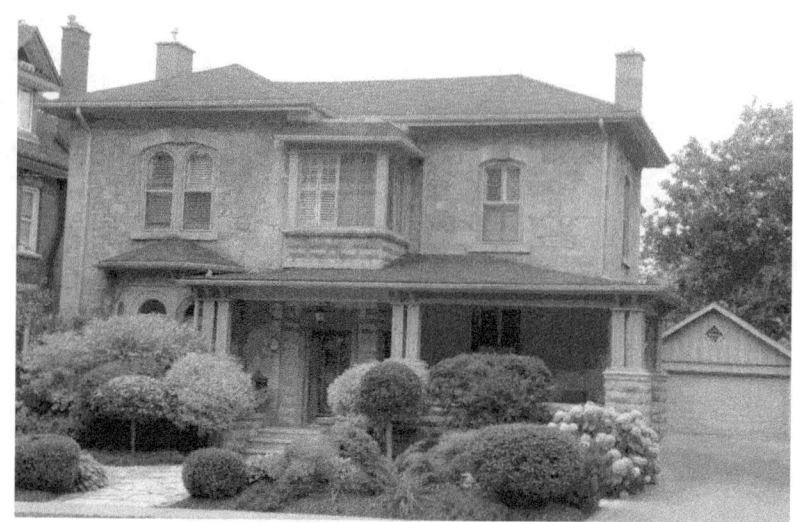

#109 – limestone

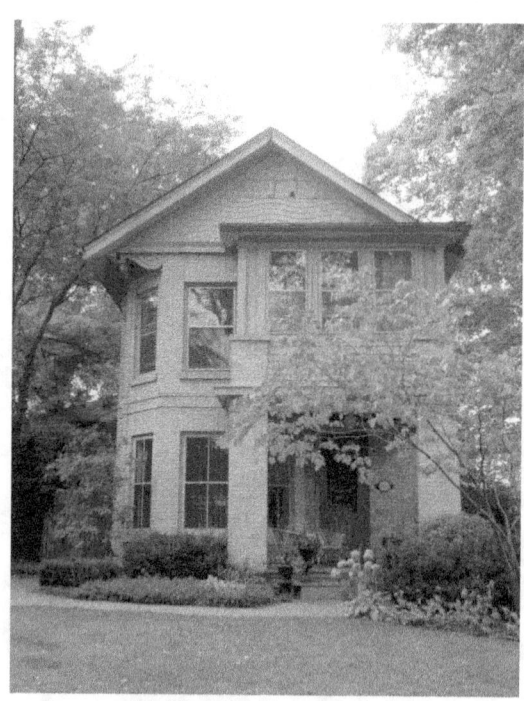

#160 – Yellow brick

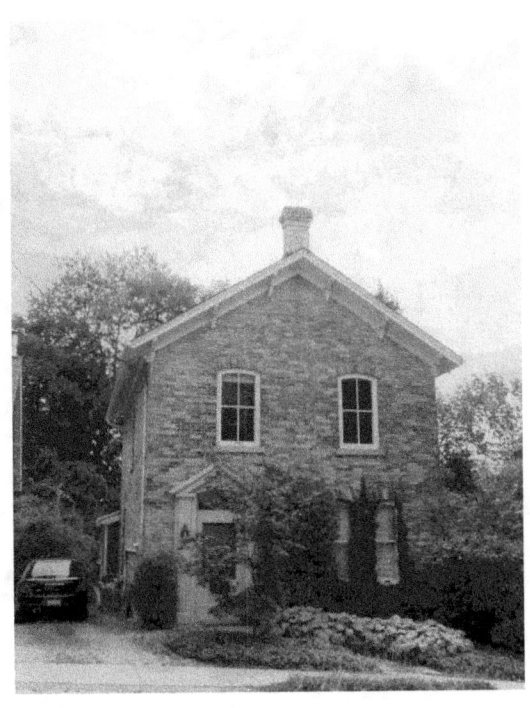

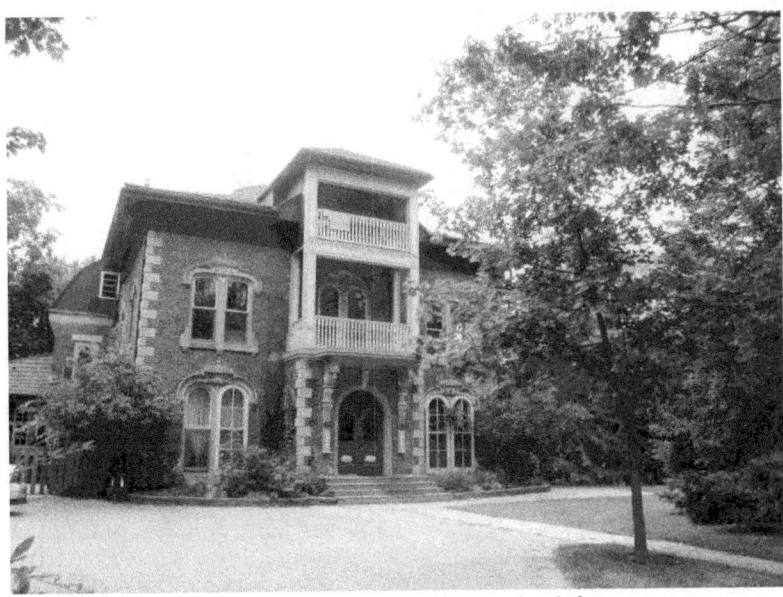

Fancy work around the windows and front entrance

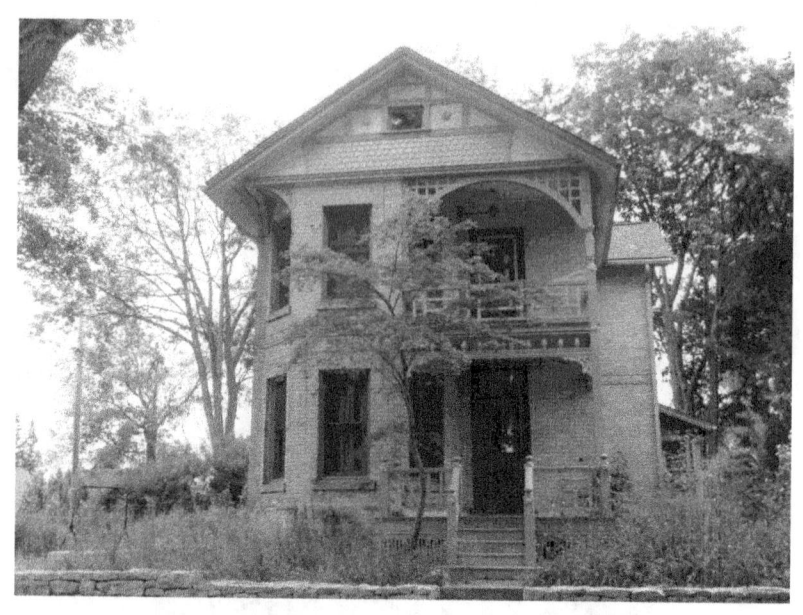

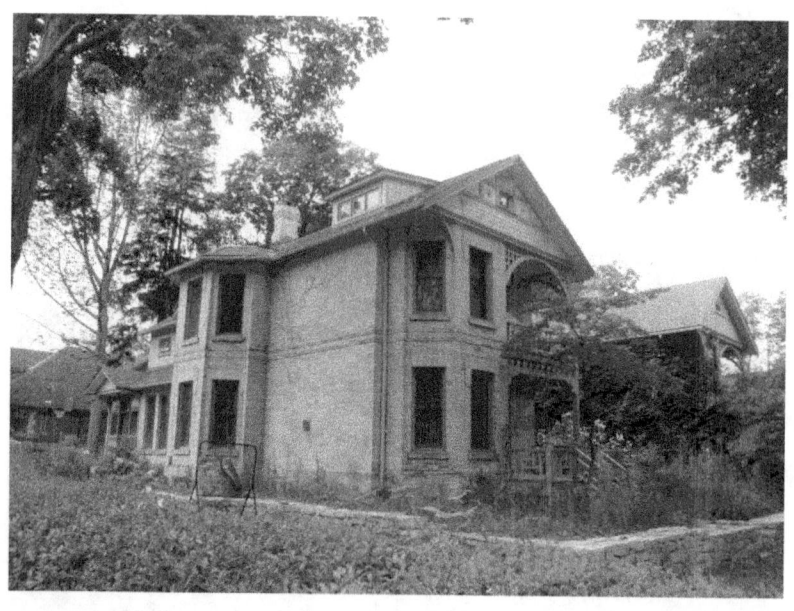

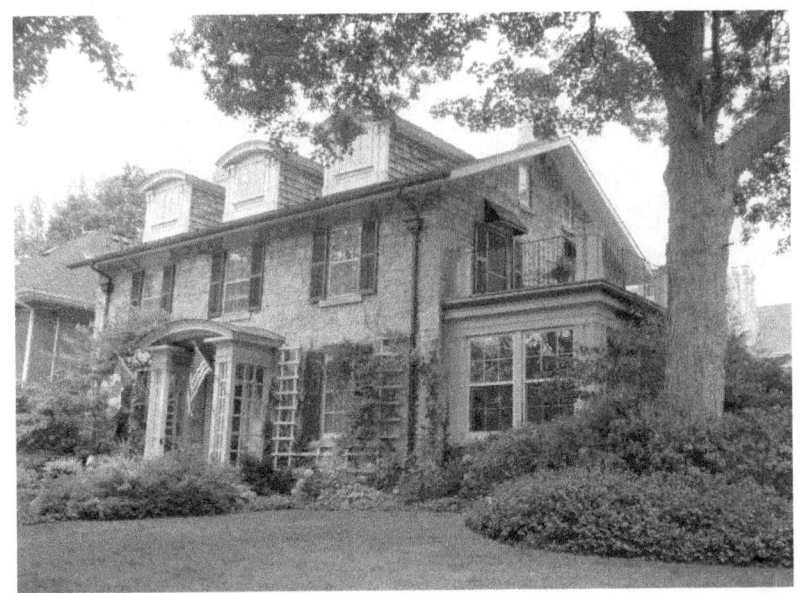

limestone

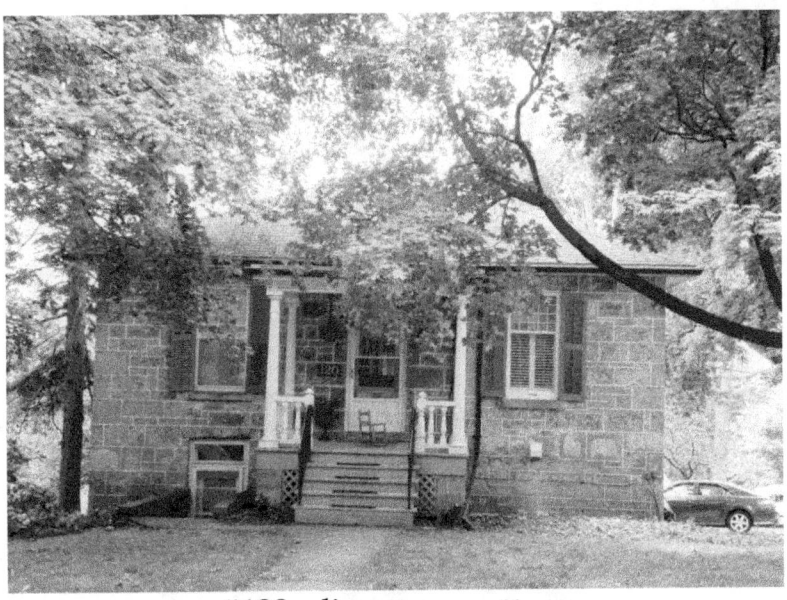

#120 – limestone cottage

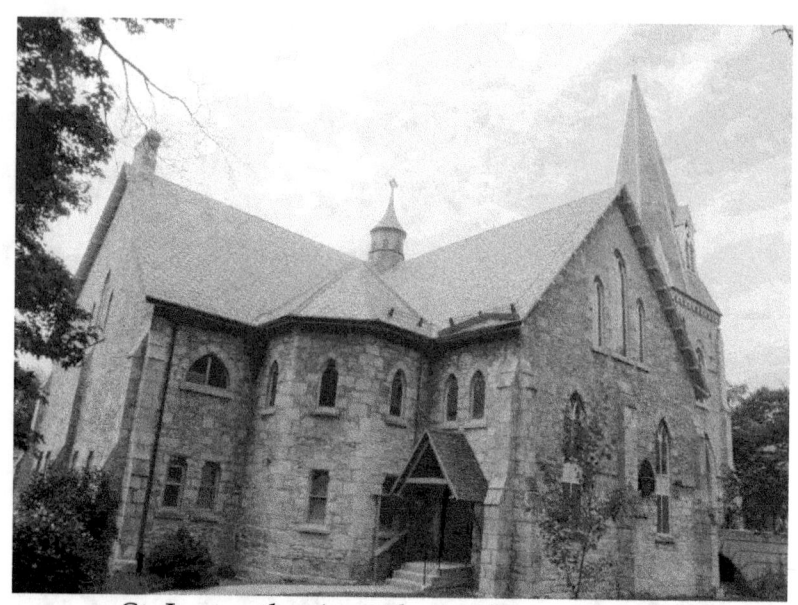

St. James the Apostle Anglican Church
86 Glasgow Street North
Built of locally quarried limestone – 1891-92

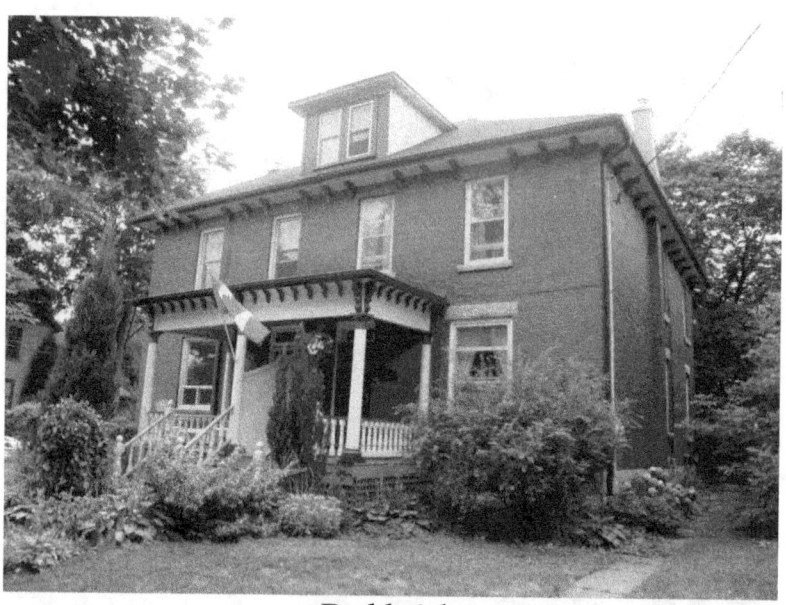

Red brick

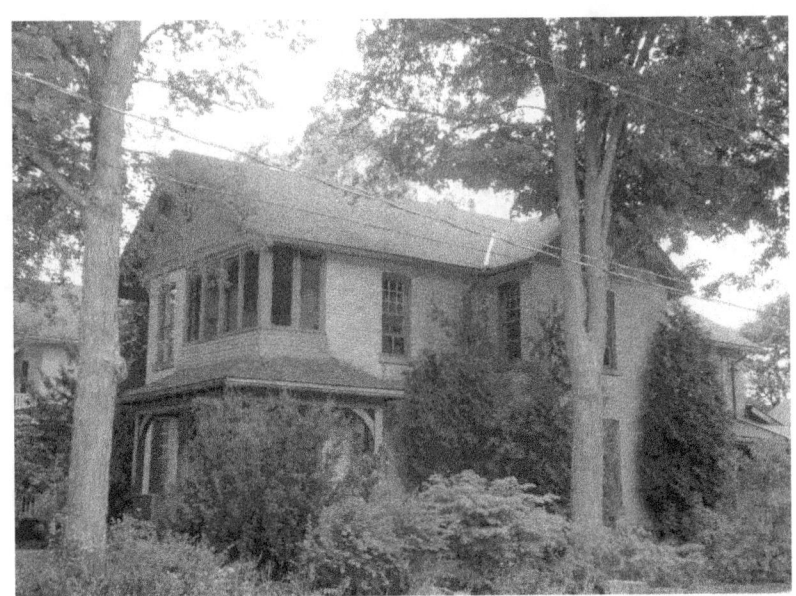

Yellow brick

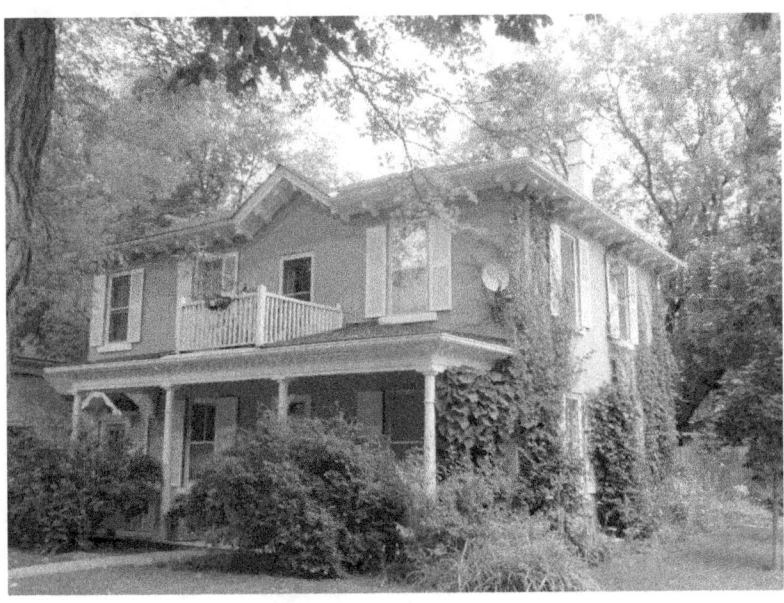

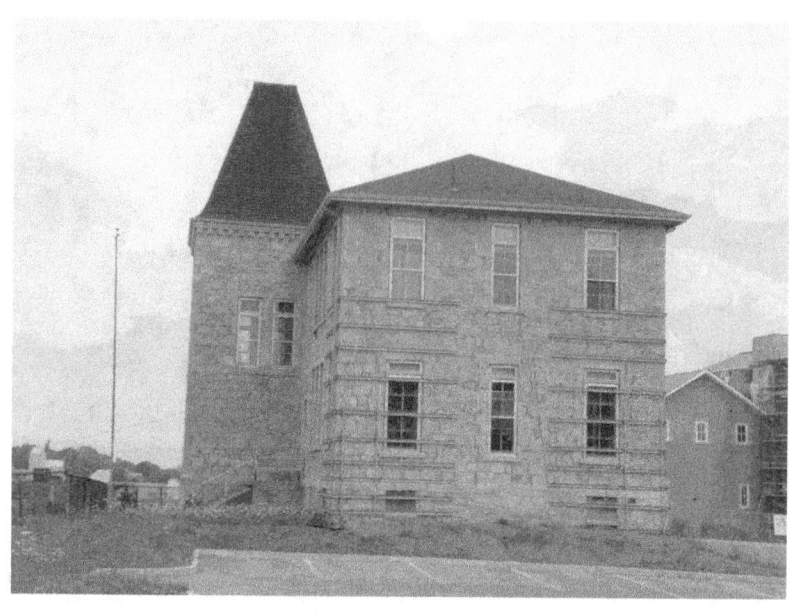

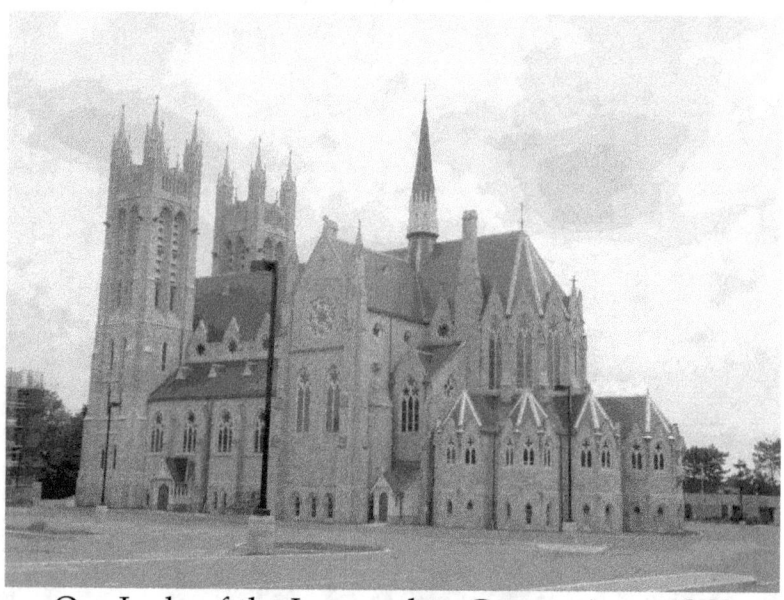

Our Lady of the Immaculate Conception – 1876
Thirteenth century French Gothic style

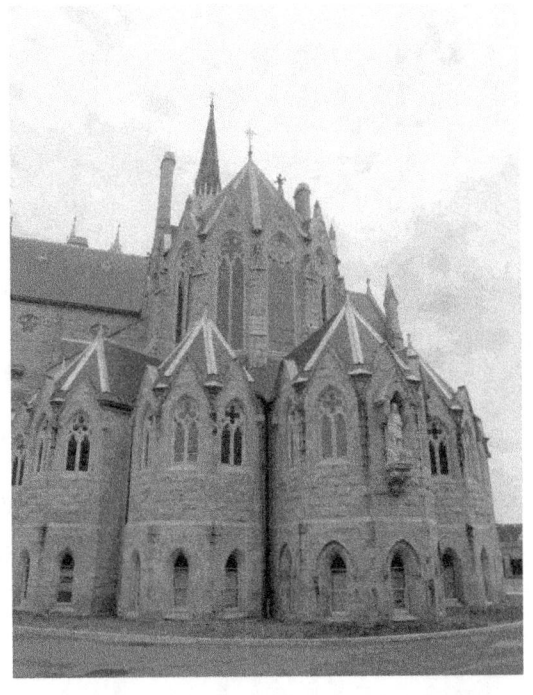

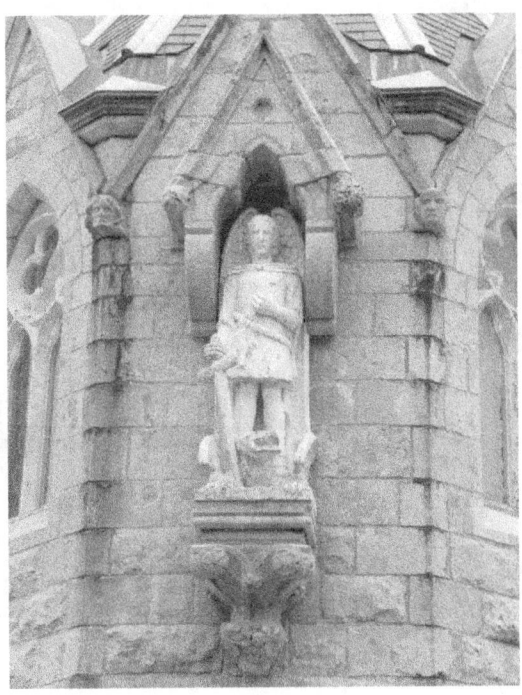

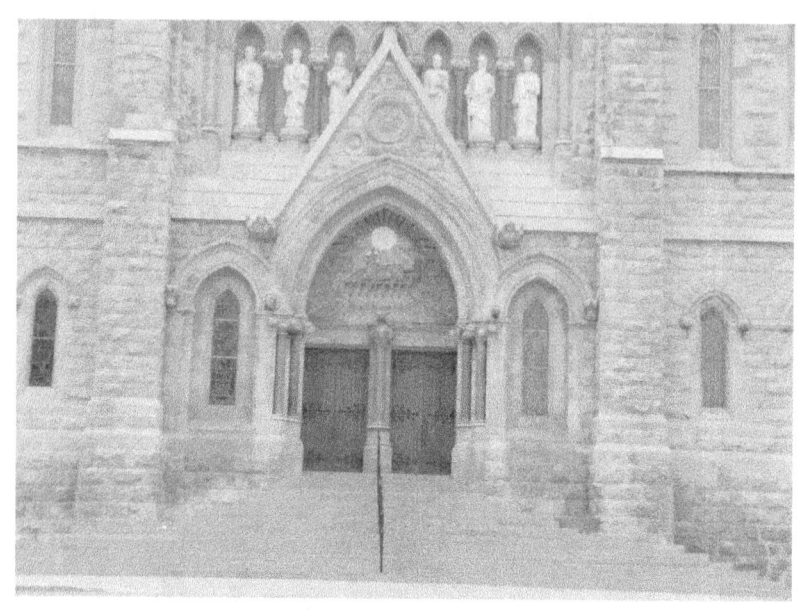

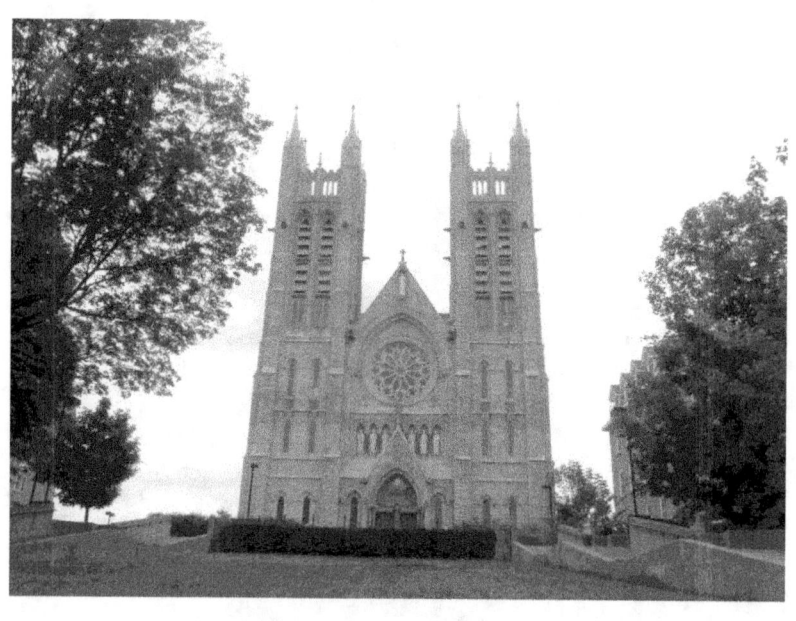

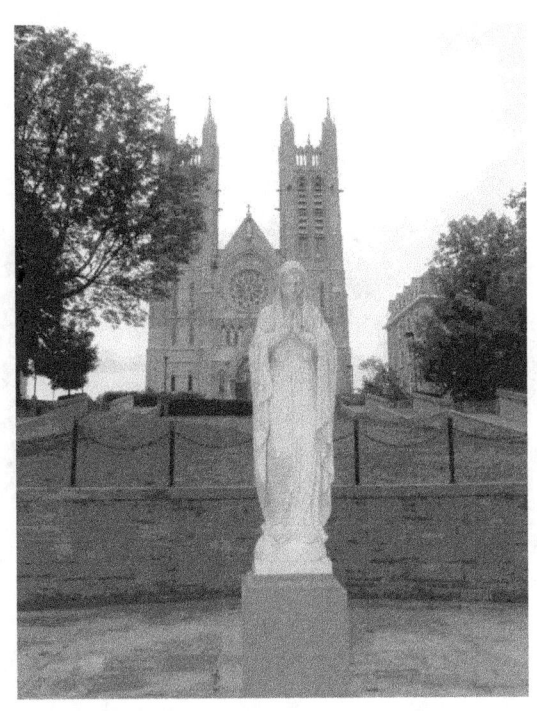

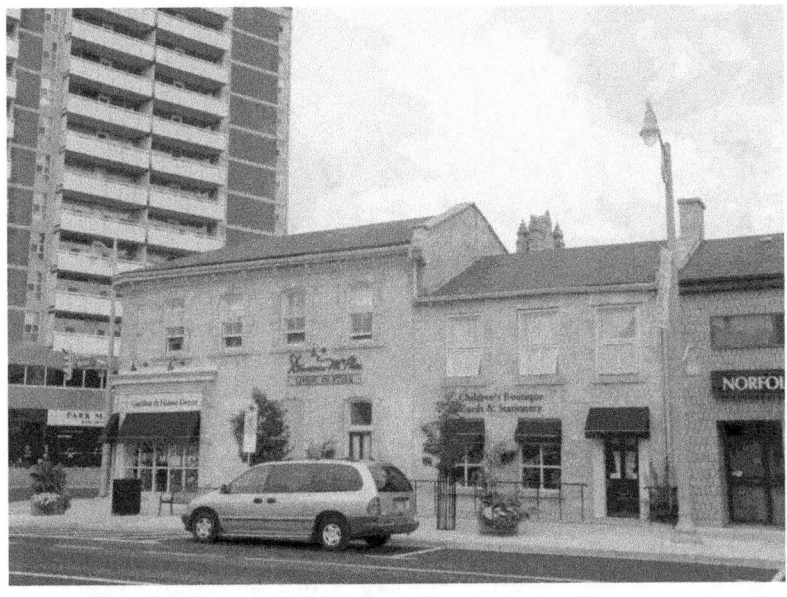

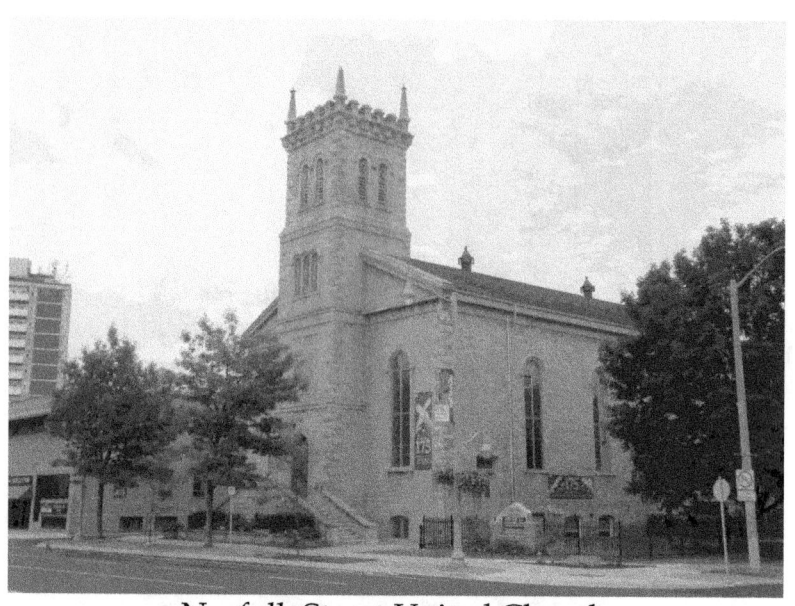

Norfolk Street United Church
1836-2011 – 175 years
(Wesleyan Methodist Church A.D. 1855)

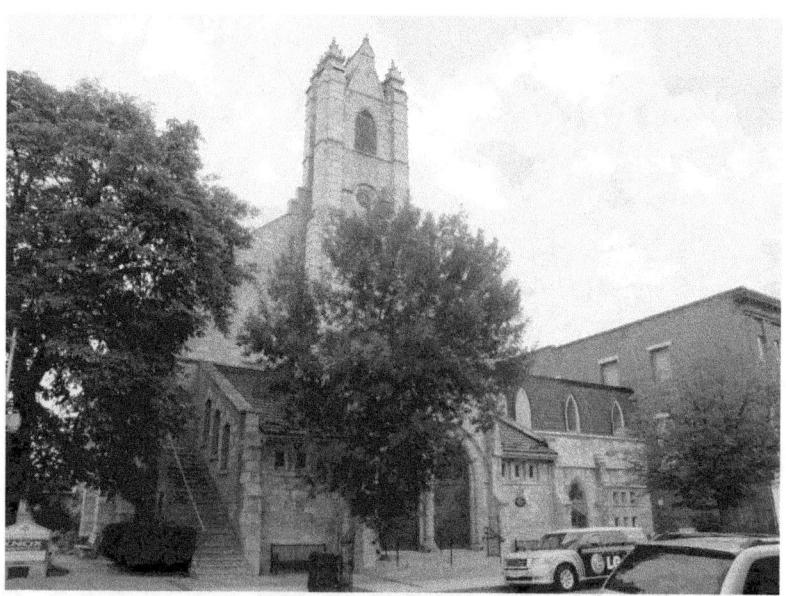

Knox Presbyterian Church established 1844
20 Quebec Street

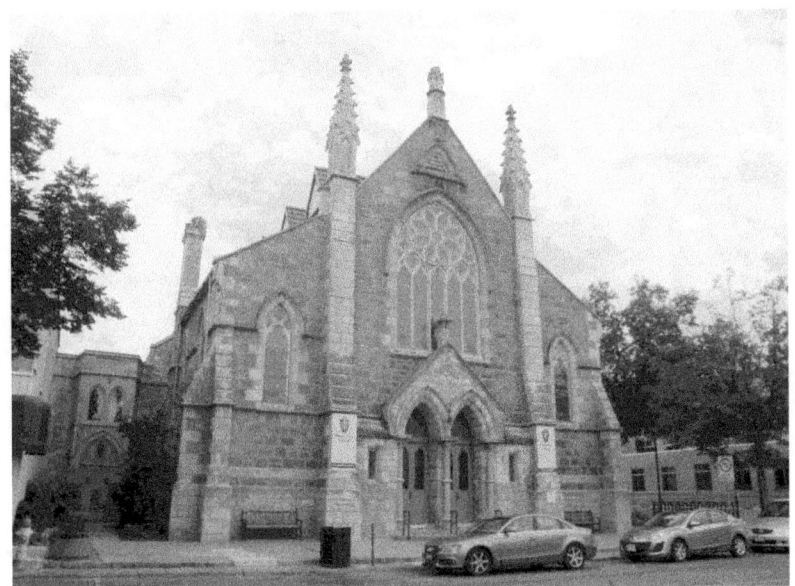

Royal City Church – 50 Quebec Street

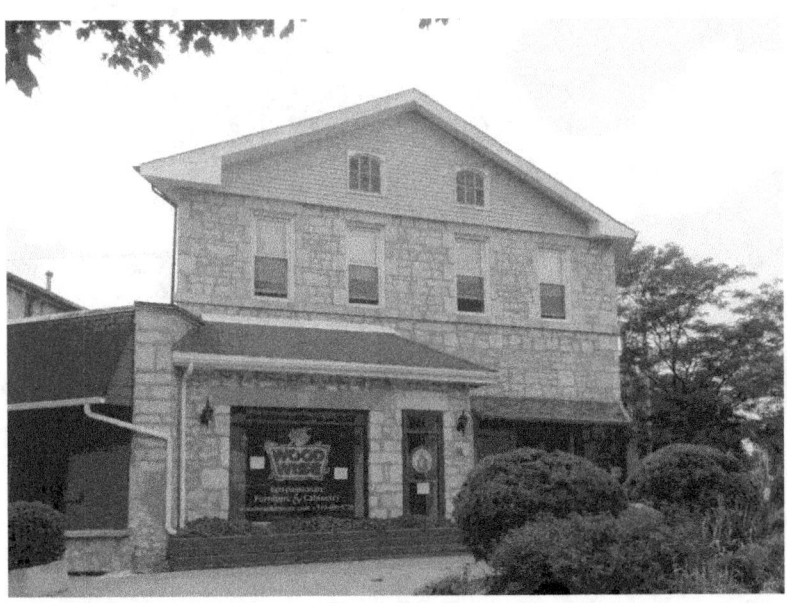

limestone

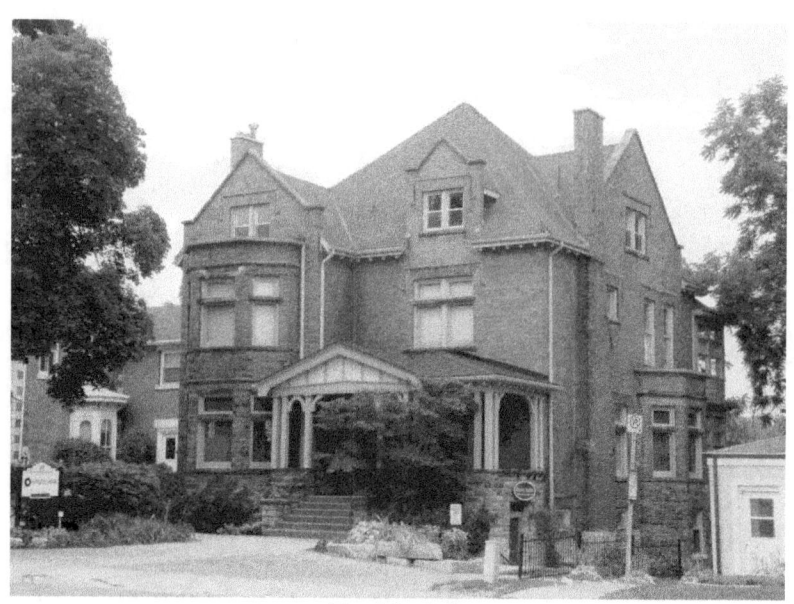

Red brick

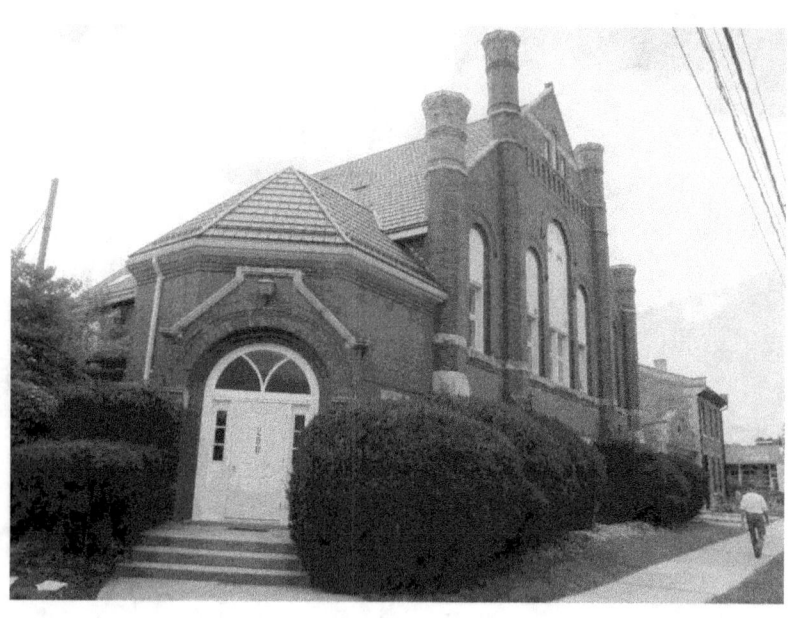

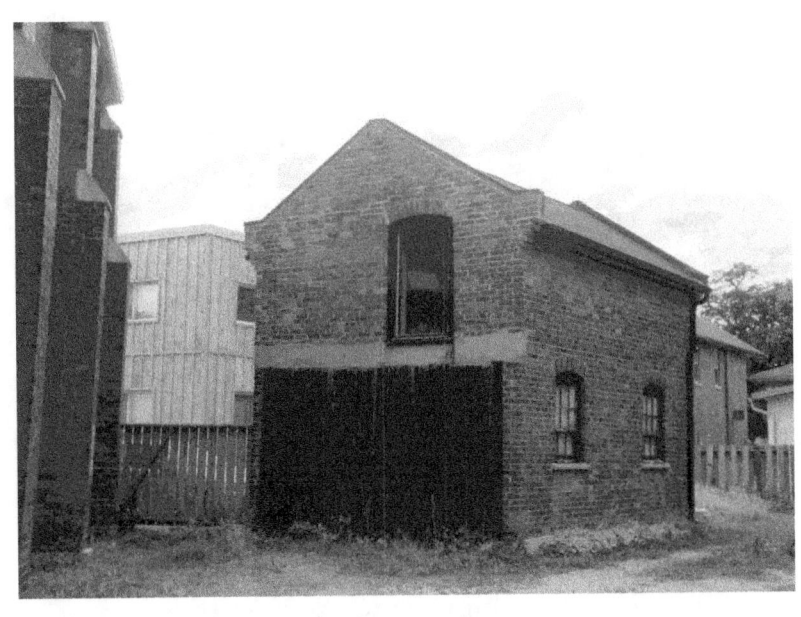

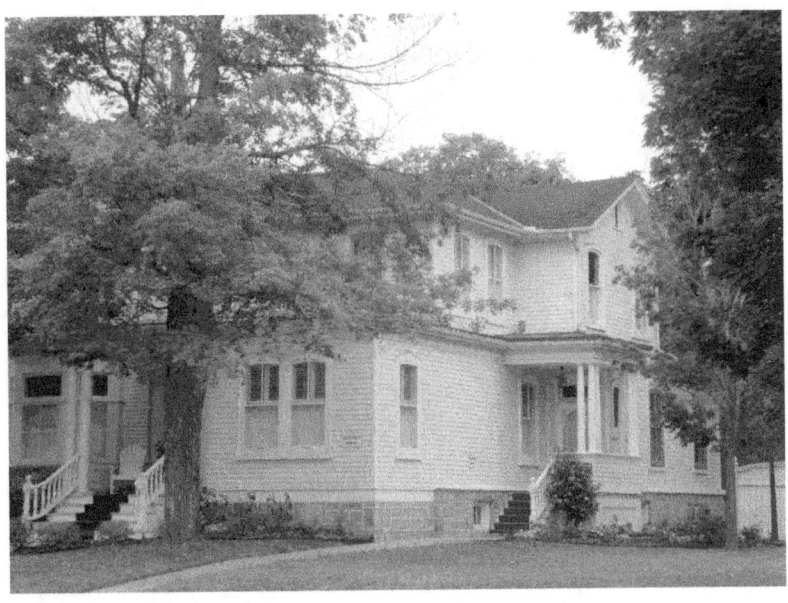

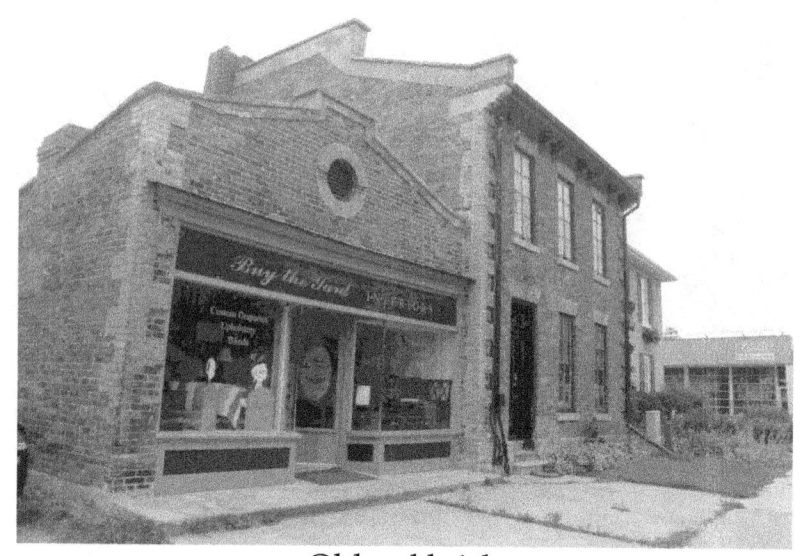

Old red brick

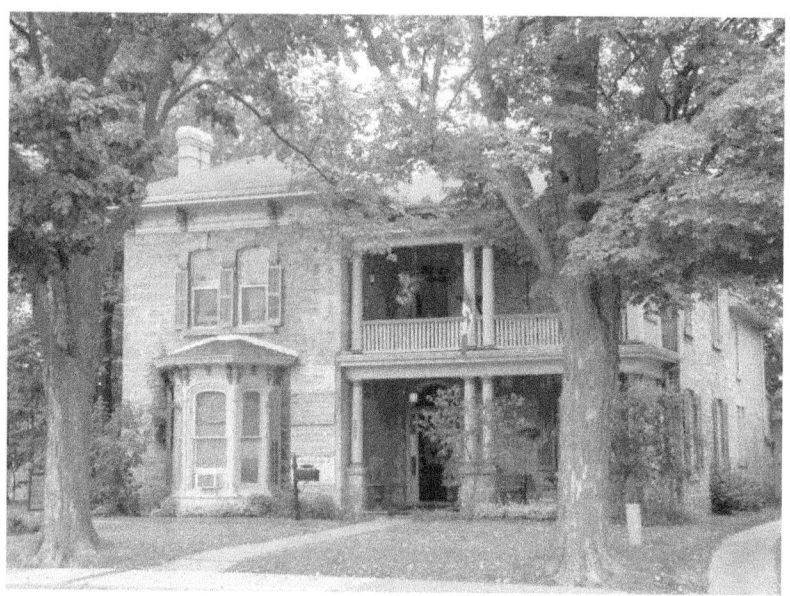

#221 – limestone

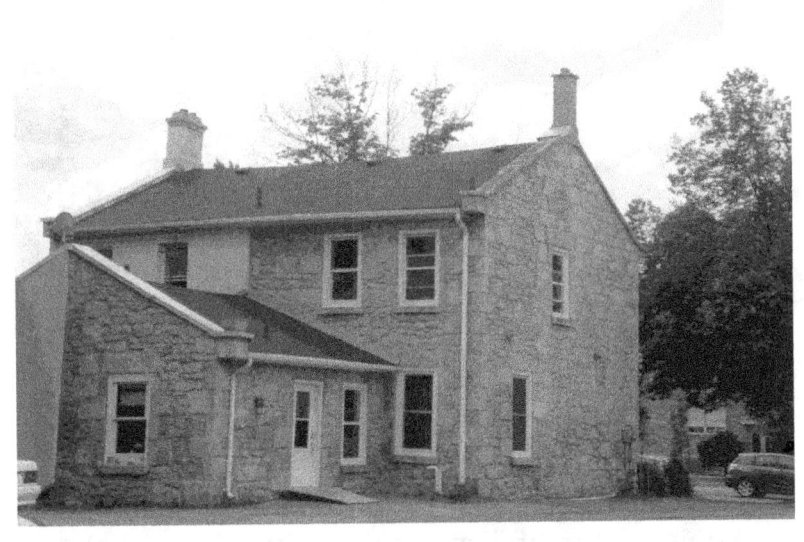

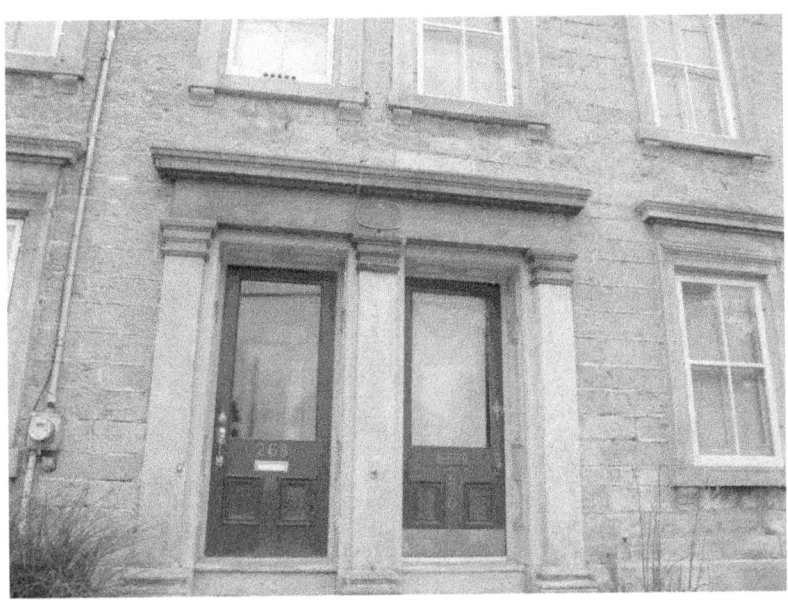

268-270 Woolwich Street

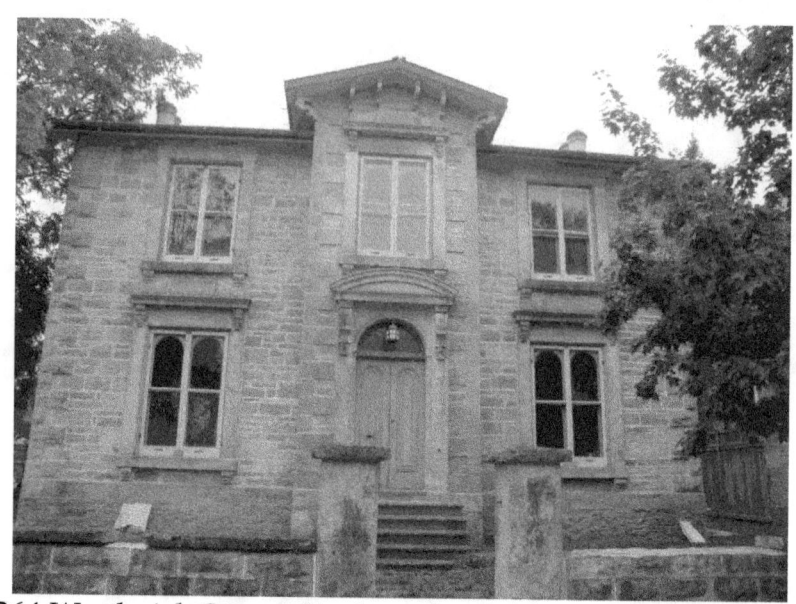

264 Woolwich Street displays the richly-carved Italianate
ornamentation of the mid-19th century – in local limestone

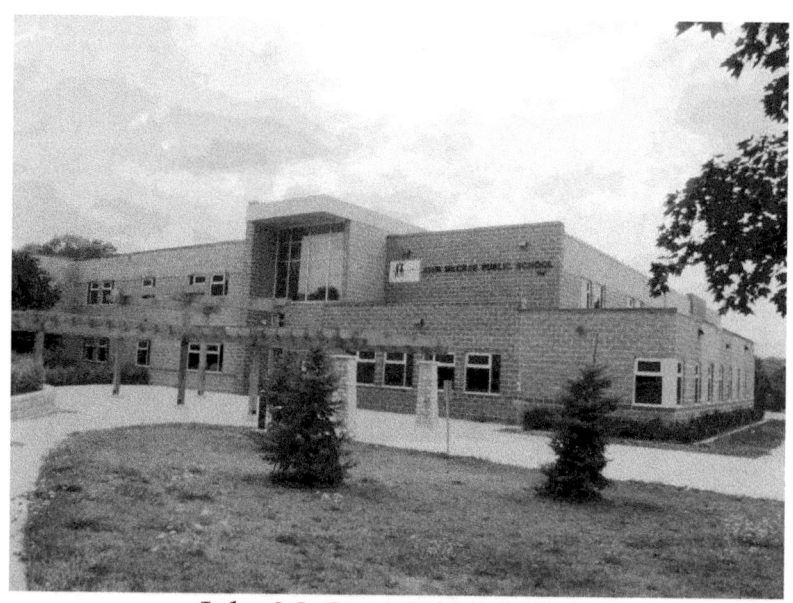

John McCrae Public School
where Grandma Todd was caretaker

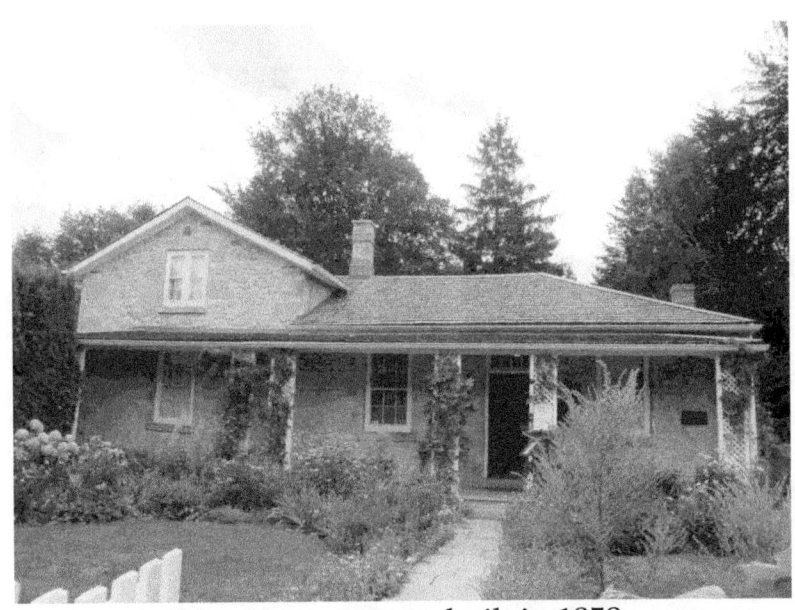

Limestone cottage built in 1858,
trellised verandah, cedar shingle roof
John McCrae born here on November 30, 1872
He wrote "In Flanders Fields"

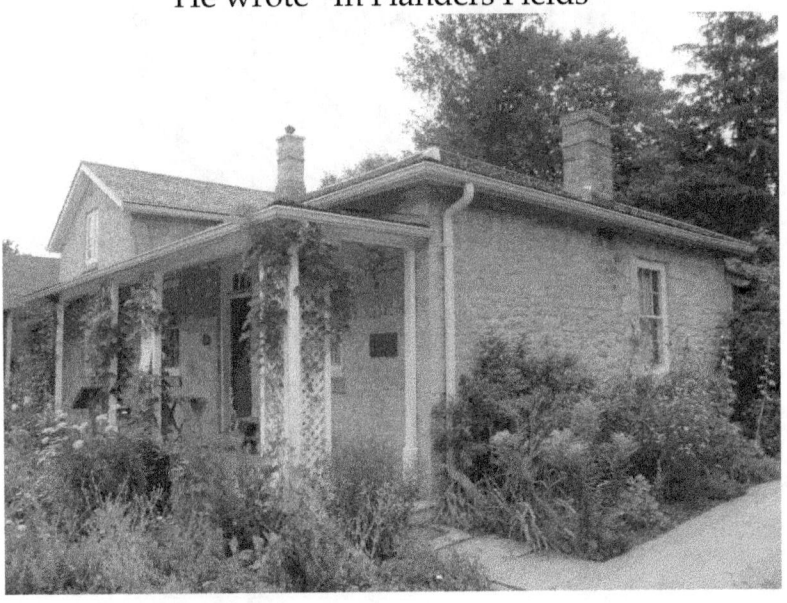

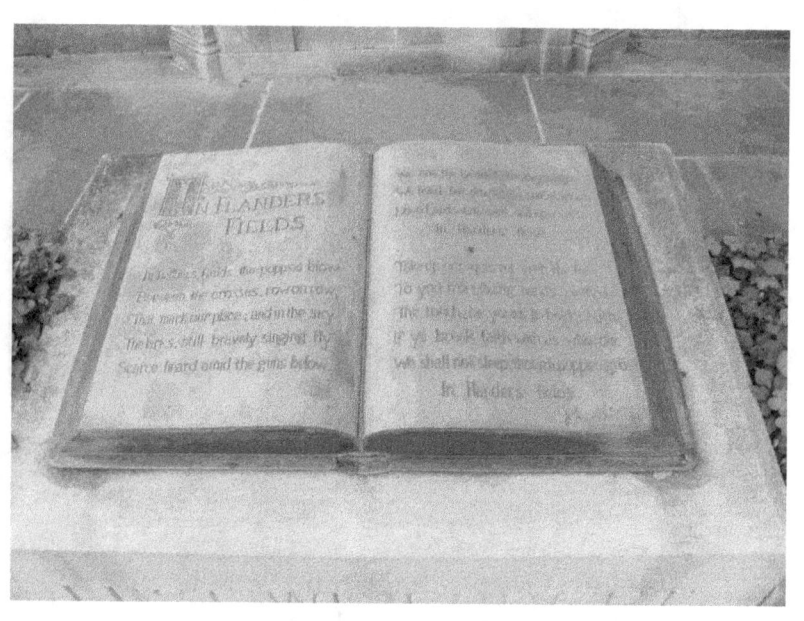

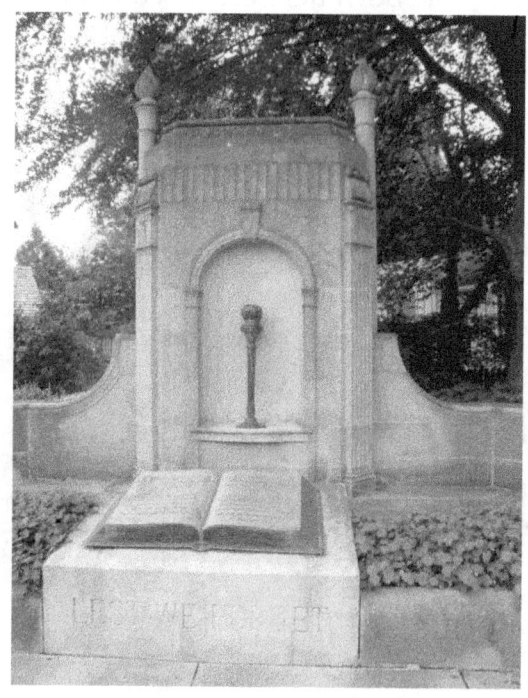

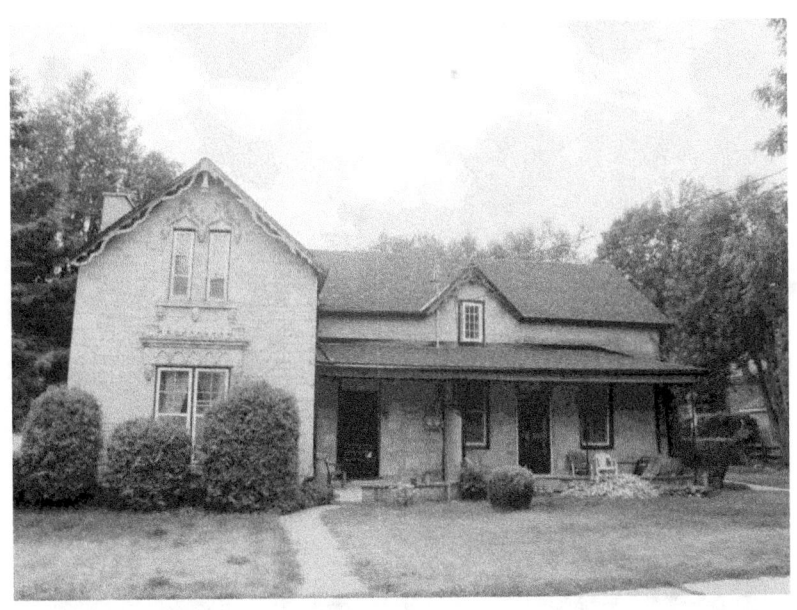

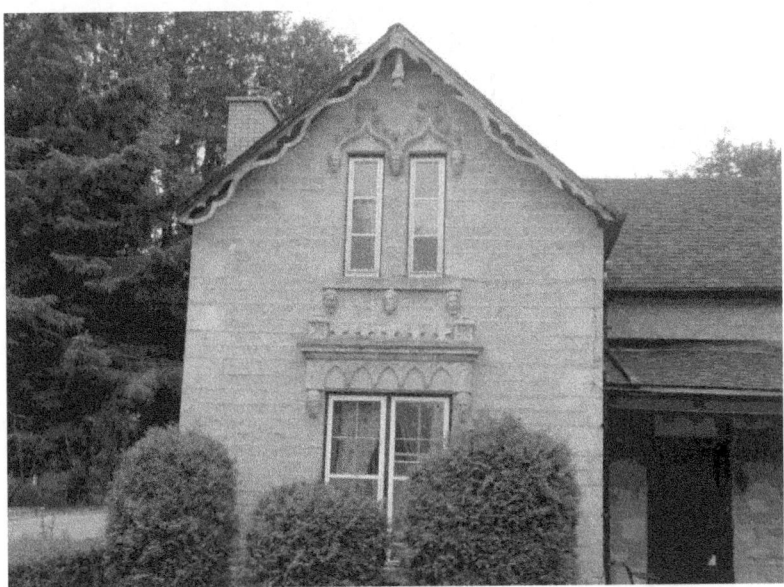

Human heads

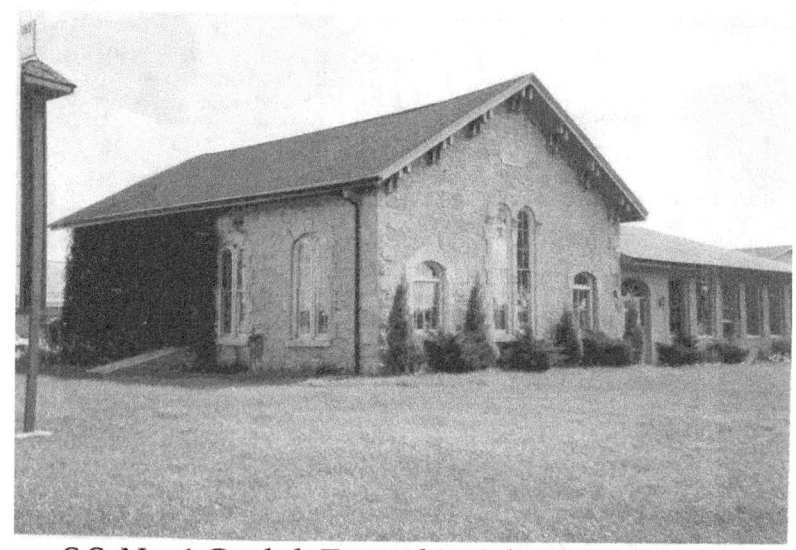

S.S. No. 1 Guelph Township School – A.D. 1873
Where I attended Grades 1 to 6 from 1957-63
Limestone, paired cornice brackets

# University of Guelph

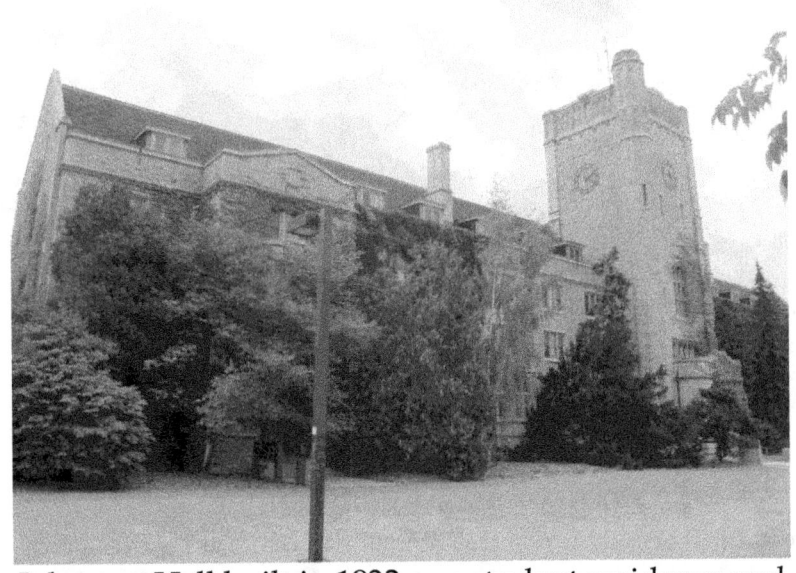

Johnston Hall built in 1932 as a student residence and administrative offices, named after the first principal

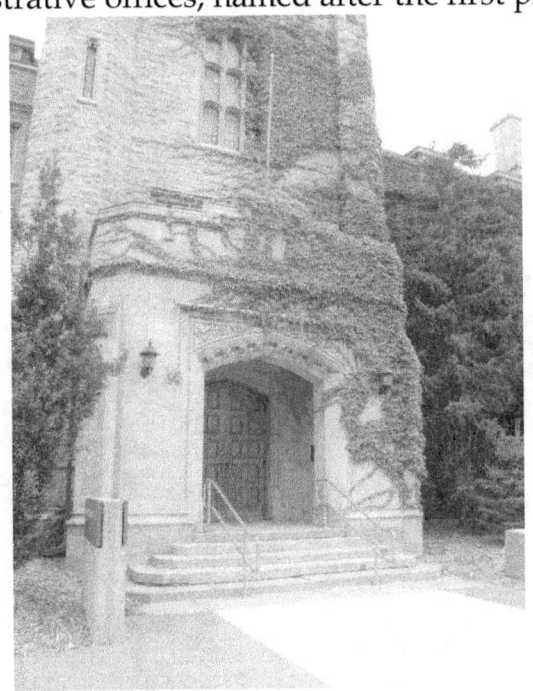

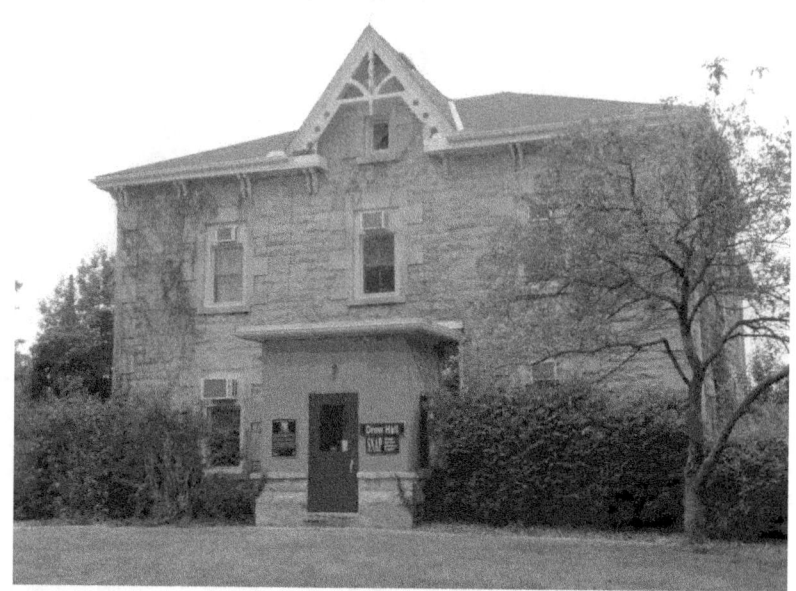

Drew Hall constructed in 1882 as the official residence of the Bursar, now used as offices for Hospitality Services

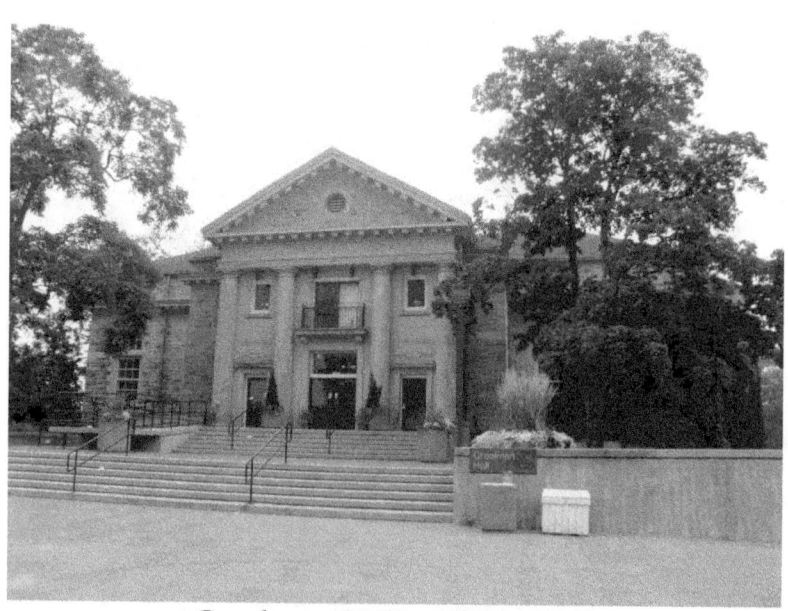

Creelman Hall – dining hall

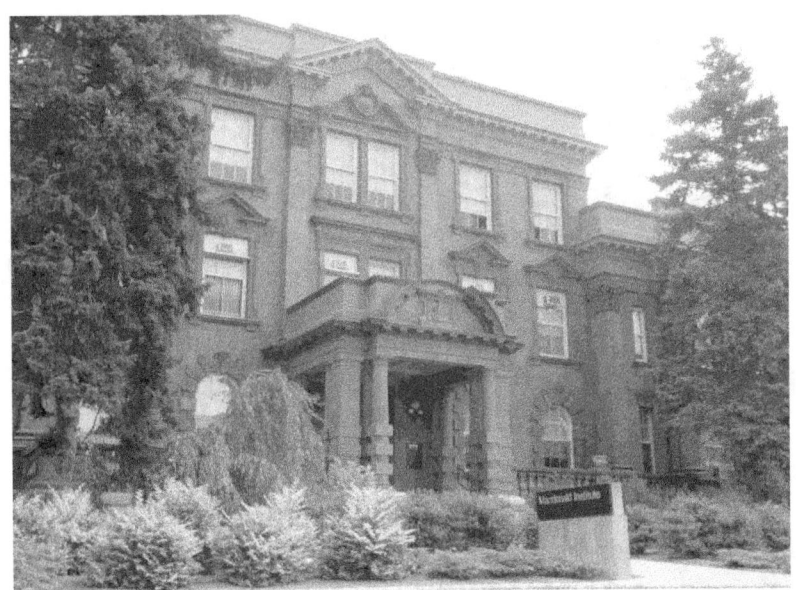

Opened in 1903, Macdonald Institute was co-founded by
Adelaide Hoodless and Sir William Macdonald, initially for
instruction for young women in nature study, manual
training, domestic science and domestic art

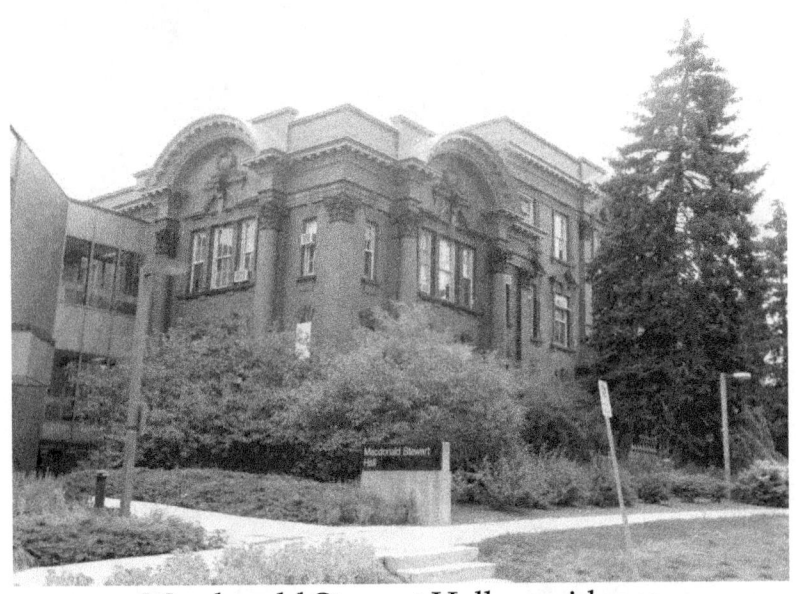

Macdonald Stewart Hall – residence

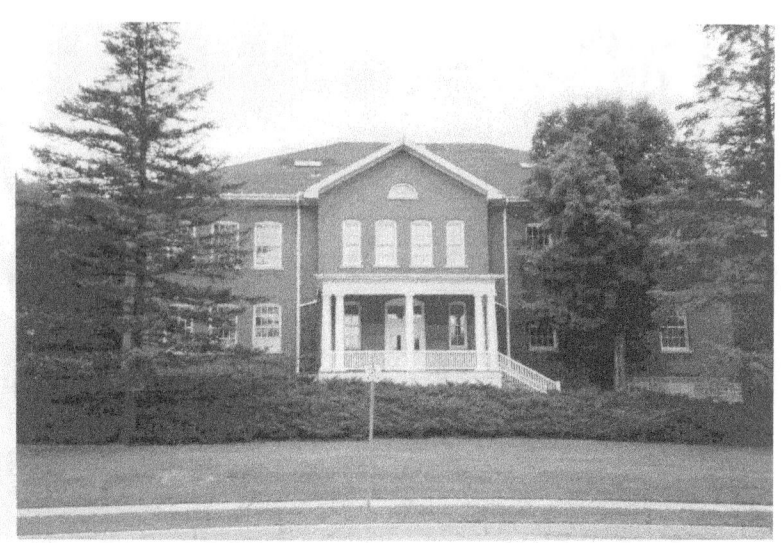

Macdonald Consolidated School where I attended Grade 7
– it closed in 1972 and reopened as
The Macdonald Stewart Art Institute

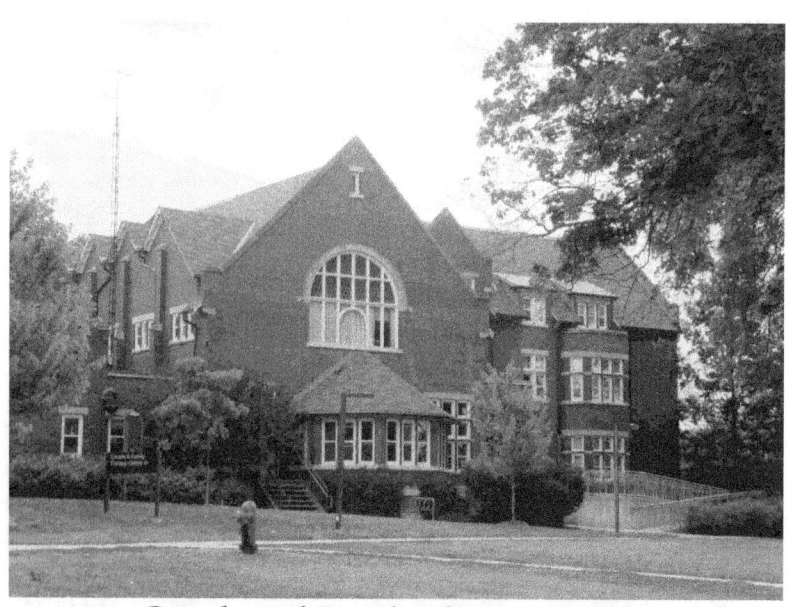

Couple and Family Therapy Centre

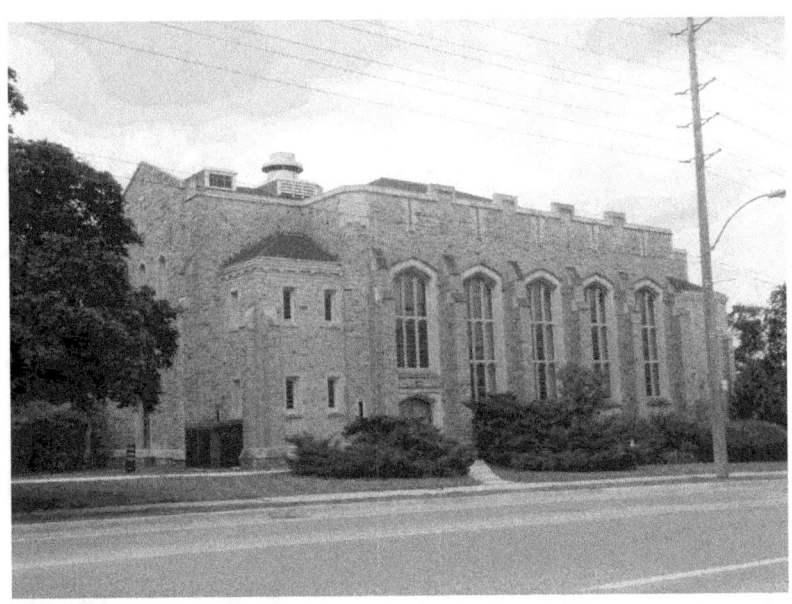

War Memorial Hall built in June 1924 as a lecture hall to honour students who had enlisted and died in World War I

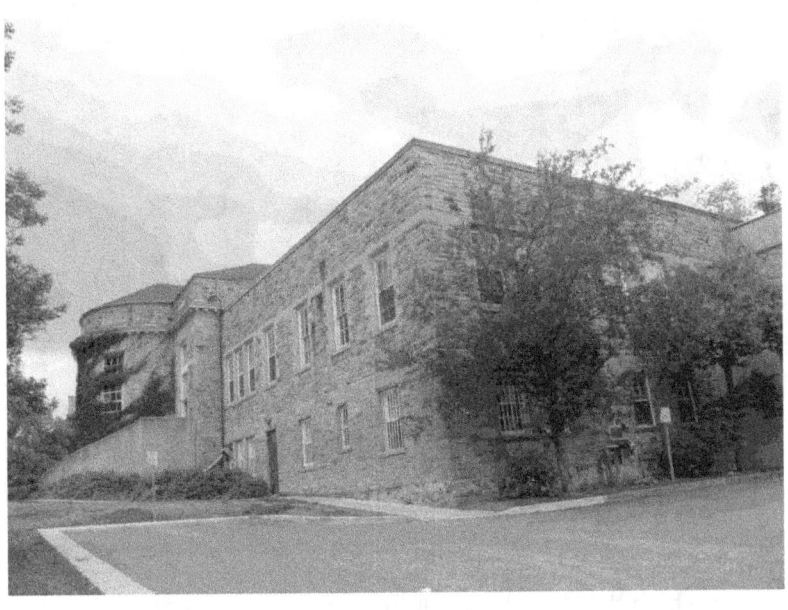

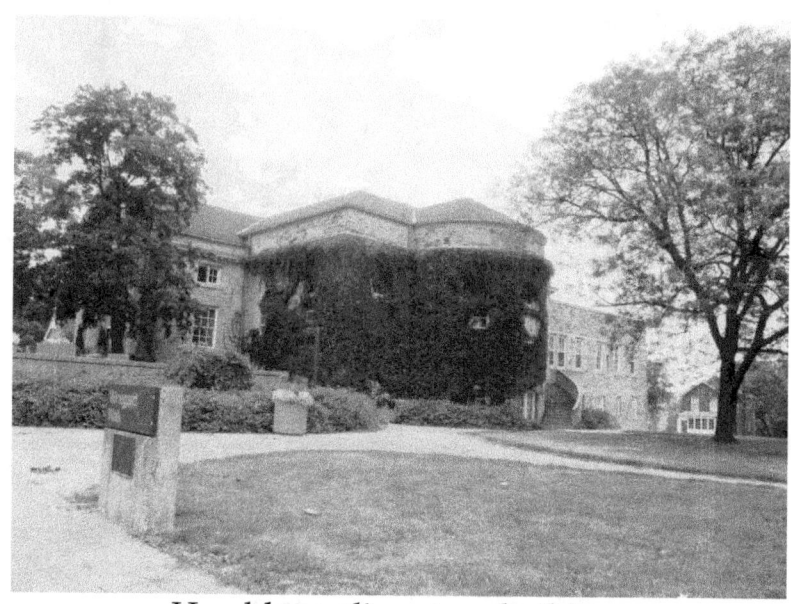

Hand-hewn limestone building

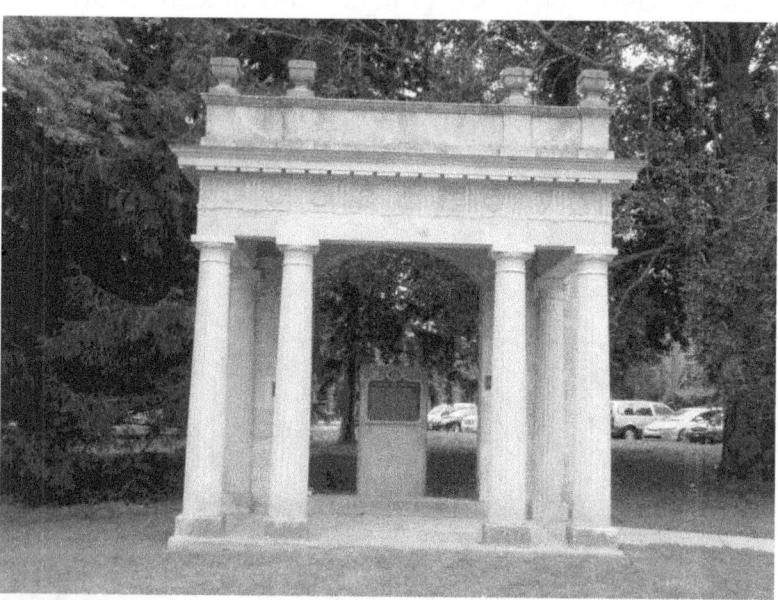

This portico was the entrance of the Frederick W. Stone farmhouse, the building in which the first classes of the Ontario School of Agriculture were held on May 1, 1874. 56 generations of students passed through this portal from 1874-1930.

# Moffat

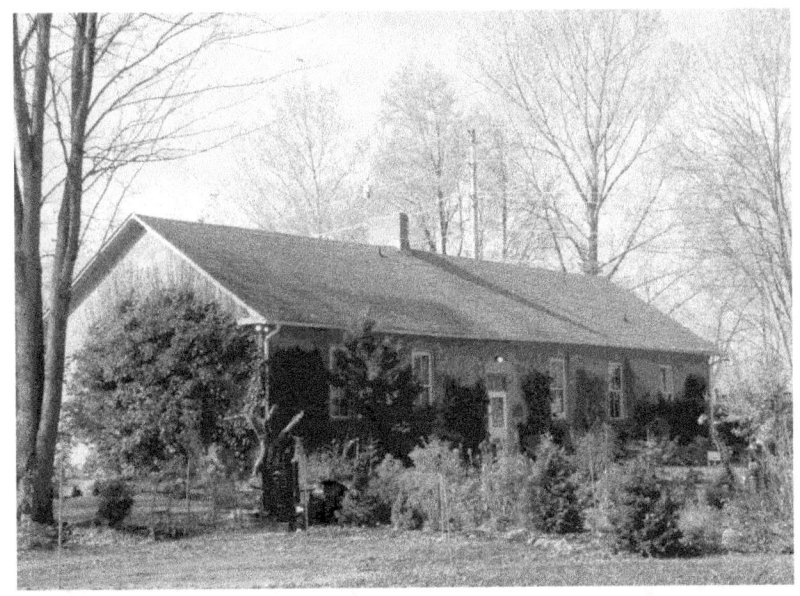

S.S. No. 3 School, Moffat – built in 1870

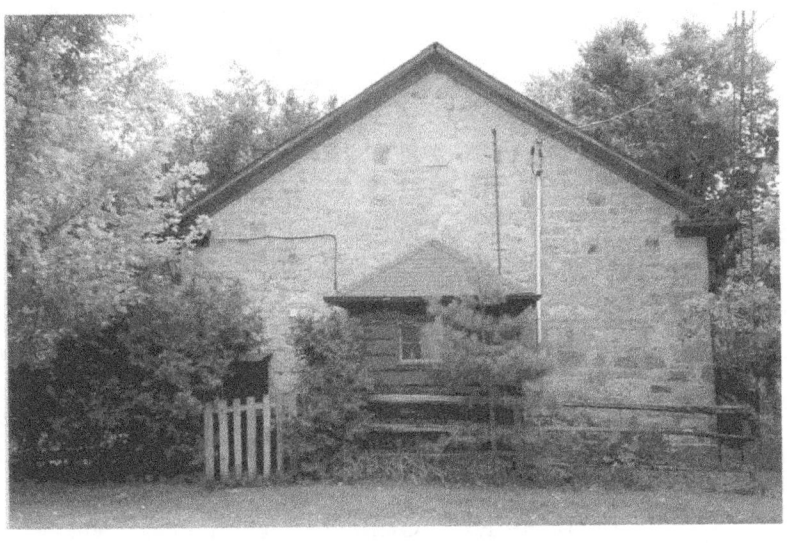

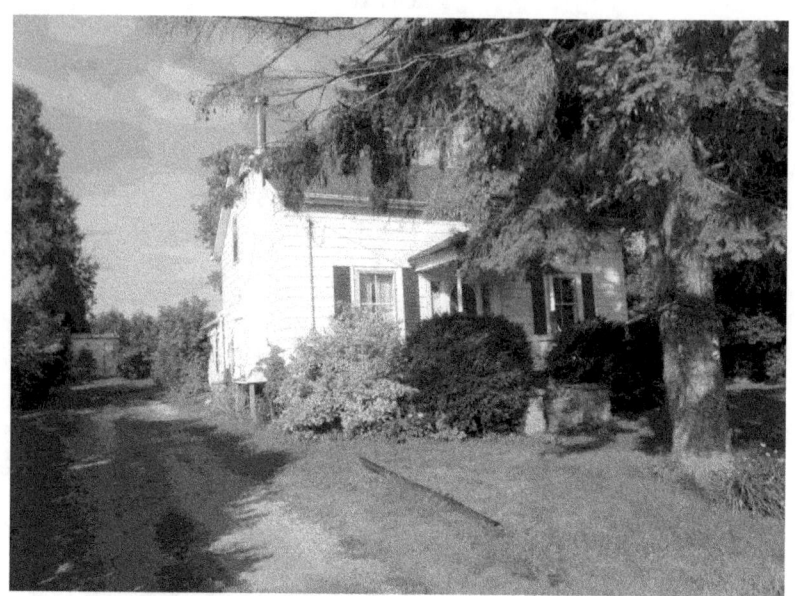

The house we lived in 1954-1956

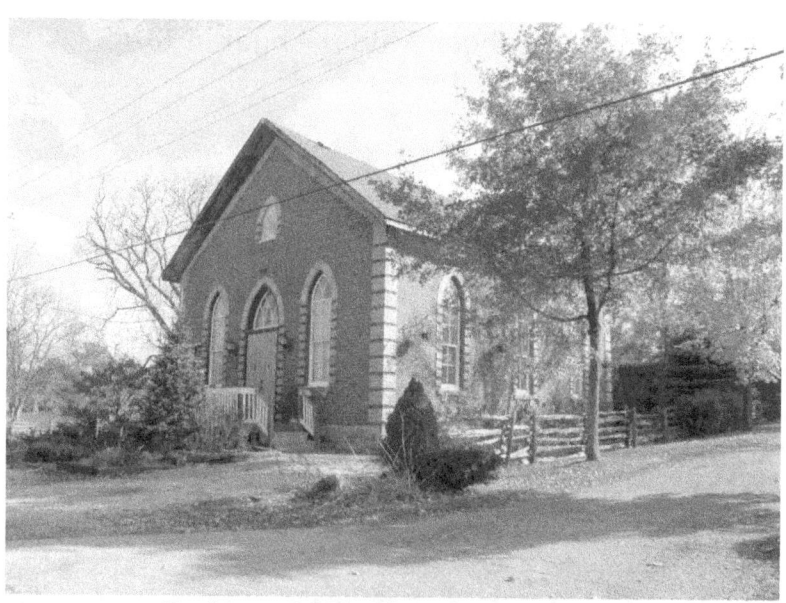

Bethany M.E. Church A.D. 1877

www.ingramcontent.com/pod-product-compliance
Lightning Source LLC
Chambersburg PA
CBHW071230170526
45165CB00003B/1060